Immigrants and Modern Racism

Immigrants and Modern Racism

REPRODUCING INEQUALITY

Beth Frankel Merenstein

LYNNE
RIENNER
PUBLISHERS

BOULDER
LONDON

Published in the United States of America in 2008 by
Lynne Rienner Publishers, Inc.
1800 30th Street, Boulder, Colorado 80301
www.rienner.com

and in the United Kingdom by
Lynne Rienner Publishers, Inc.
3 Henrietta Street, Covent Garden, London WC2E 8LU

Library of Congress Cataloging-in-Publication Data
Merenstein, Beth Frankel, 1971–
  Immigrants and modern racism: reproducing inequality/Beth Frankel
Merenstein.
  Includes bibliographical references and index.
  ISBN: 978-1-58826-573-9 (hardcover: alk. paper)
  1. Immigrants—United States—Social conditions. 2. Immigrants—United
States—Psychology. 3. Racism—United States. 4. Racism—Psychological
aspects—United States. 5. United States—Race relations. 6. United
States—Ethnic relations. I. Title.
JV6475.M47 2008
305.800973—dc22

                                                    2008012822

British Cataloguing in Publication Data
A Cataloguing in Publication record for this book
is available from the British Library.

Printed and bound in the United States of America

Printed on 30% postconsumer recycled paper

The paper used in this publication meets the requirements
of the American National Standard for Permanence of
Paper for Printed Library Materials Z39.48-1992.

5 4 3 2 1

Contents

Acknowledgments

THE ONLY WAY FOR ANY BOOK to see completion is through the concerted efforts of a number of people. This book was no exception. In particular, I would like to thank Leanne Anderson at Lynne Rienner Publishers, whose tireless dedication and unwavering support sustained the belief that an end was actually in sight. I also want to thank the anonymous reviewers for their thoughtful and insightful suggestions. Their ideas were invaluable as I shaped my manuscript into a stronger and more cohesive book.

Although I did not study sociology at Clark University, Shelly Tenenbaum piqued my curiosity in the discipline and first introduced me to the idea that not only could I learn about race and ethnic relations in this country, but I could teach about it as well. At the University of Connecticut, Ken Neubeck, Ron Taylor, Bandana Purkayastha, and Davita Glasberg nurtured my intellectual development, challenged me to think about issues of race and immigration in new ways, and made a commitment to mentoring that continues to leave a lasting impression. At Central Connecticut State University, the entire Sociology Department deserves my thanks and gratitude. In differing ways they provided much needed laughter, a sounding board for ideas, and a true commitment to the notion of collegiality. I especially want to thank Heide Tarchini for all her assistance in making sure the book reached the publisher at all stages of the process.

I also want to thank those at Literacy Volunteers of Eastern City, especially Margie Arroyo, and the numerous immigrants and support service workers who spoke to me about their thoughts, beliefs, and dreams. I can only hope I have done justice to their words.

My family deserves the most gratitude for its support through this long endeavor. Without the help and support of Barbara and Arnold Frankel, it is likely this book would have taken even longer to come to fruition. My brothers and sisters-in-law were a continual network of emotional support. They provided the right words of inquiry, encouragement, and sustenance, and lots of love and laughter. My husband and partner, Jeremy Frankel, celebrated each stage of the completed manuscript and never doubted that the finished product would be worth the long hours and many weekends I labored. He has given me much to be thankful for in life, is my strongest supporter, and continues to remind me to laugh, relax, and enjoy the show.

Finally, I dedicate this book to four people. First, to my parents, Joel and Nancy Merenstein, for their love, kindness, intelligence, fierce loyalty, and unequivocal support. They instilled in me a desire to right wrongs, to be the best that I can possibly be, and to never give up on what I want from life; without a doubt, I am where I am today because of them. Second, to my amazing children, Jordan Sarah and Maya Rose Frankel, who were glimmerings on the horizon when this book began and who have grown right alongside it. They are the best thing to ever happen to me, reminding me that while there may be violence and anger in the world, there are also beautiful and loving things. As long as we can hold onto that knowledge, the world truly can become a better place.

Immigrants and Modern Racism

1

Learning Race: Becoming an "American"

WHO IS AN "AMERICAN"? IN THE early 1900s, arguments abounded about who was a real American and who could become one. Centered on issues of race, citizenship, and immigration, we have never completely left those arguments behind. Now, in the early years of a new century, we are again in the midst of discussions about what it means to be an American. The contemporary political debates, media conversations, and public discourse focusing on issues of immigration, both legal and illegal, are really looking at issues about Americanization—about who gets included in this definition, about how some are considered "real Americans" and others are not. What does it mean now to be an American?

The majority of native-born Americans believe that to become American, an immigrant must fully assimilate into this new culture and society. A primary focus of this required assimilation is learning the language, but opponents to immigration believe new immigrants are not acculturating in other ways as well. For example, some towns and cities across the country are instituting ordinances against overcrowding in apartments and homes, believing this will deter immigrants from having "too many" people living together. The focus on perceived cultural differences between immigrant and native-born Americans is often a distinction of race, couched in cultural terminology. However, while new immigrants are expected and, in fact, even demanded to become Americanized, they are also encouraged to retain some of their previous "ethnic ways." For example, in recent years, native-born Americans have embraced "ethnic" restaurants, such as Vietnamese, Thai, and Mexican. This schizophrenic mentality about ethnicity in the United States affects not only the way new immigrants see themselves and their children, but also the way they see others.

Immigrants themselves grapple with the question of who is an American on a daily basis. They often struggle with the desire to make a new life for themselves in the United States, yet retain their connections to their natal country. And as they are socialized into their new lives, their identity often changes and develops. One of the major influences on this new identity is the fact that immigrants to the United States are entering a world in which race continues to hold great importance and meaning. This highly racialized society promotes a dominant racial ideology that immigrants learn, absorb, and incorporate into their identity. Known as "modern racism," this ideology holds that everyone is treated equally, that policies ensuring equal treatment are unnecessary, that hard work will provide success, and that any lack of success comes from natural or cultural deficiencies. An essential piece to this ideology is the racial hierarchy, an ordering that places white Americans on the top, black Americans on the bottom, and leaves all others striving to find their places in between.

Previous immigrants, largely from Europe, went through a simultaneous process of becoming American and "becoming white" (Roediger 1991). The racial ideology of the time promoted a desire for white racial identity that new immigrants quickly learned. Currently, immigrants do not necessarily have this same option of becoming white, nor may they even want it. However, they are also very clear that they do not want to be black. Why and how do today's immigrants learn this? How is the process of becoming American connected to the process of learning the dominant racial ideology?

I argue that part of the process of becoming American involves taking on US values and ideologies; unfortunately, one aspect of US values and ideology is racism. Further, immigrants come to the United States, as they have for hundreds of years, seeking the American Dream. An integral part of that dream is a belief that US society is based on meritocracy. Many immigrants fervently believe that social mobility is open to anyone who works hard for it; they have to believe this, otherwise, what was the point in coming to the United States? Yet, what are today's immigrants supposed to think of the preponderance of native-born racial minorities living in poverty? Is this proof that social mobility does not exist equally for everyone? Accepting that years of oppression, discrimination, and racism are possible reasons for the great number of racial minorities living in lower socioeconomic status challenges new immigrants' beliefs and notions about life in the United States. Accepting that some people face discrimination would mean having to alter or even discard the ideology of the American Dream. Instead, one of the most prominent themes to emerge from my research is that many immigrants, rather than accept the idea that racism exists, acquiesce to the dominant ideologies that for many on the bottom, their generally low social status is due to their own lack of hard work and to their own failures.

Immigrants learn these ideologies from the racial social structure surrounding them, from the culture expressed in this structure, and from their own racial habitus (the experiences and beliefs of those around them, combined with their own experiences and beliefs). In this book, I explore how these three elements work together to make "racial beings" out of immigrants: how they come to see the racial structure, how that affects their own identities and interactions with others, and, finally, how they themselves affect this racial structure by accepting, altering, or challenging the dominant ideologies in a process I call "racial reproduction." Before I fully explain this model of racial reproduction, however, it is important to explain the concept of social reproduction and how my ideas of racial reproduction developed from this very important and useful earlier model.

Social Reproduction

Individualism and achievement attained through personal hard work are ever-present ideologies in the United States, ideologies that promote the common belief in the possibility of social mobility. Unfortunately, as decades of quantitative sociological, economic, and political studies have reported, the reality is that individuals tend to stay within the social class into which they are born (Lampard 2007, Crompton 2006). This tendency is known as "social reproduction" (MacLeod 1995). While these quantitative studies are extremely useful for documenting the realities of our social class system, it is primarliy from qualitative studies, such as MacLeod's (1995), that we can understand how this process occurs.

A social reproduction framework can illustrate "the specific mechanisms and processes that contribute to the inter-generational transmission of social inequality" (MacLeod 1995:7). This framework can be divided into three levels of analysis: social structure, culture, and agency/individual. These levels work together to describe the overall reproduction process. Additionally, social reproduction theory can highlight not only the barriers to social mobility, but also how some individuals are not completely blocked from attaining mobility. When a few token individuals make it through these barriers, the predominant belief in widespread social mobility is ensured (Langston 2001, Kahlenberg 1996, Newman 1999, 1993).

Looking at how individuals experience and respond to such constricting boundaries as poor quality education and the limited opportunity for class mobility, and how they accept or resist their position and the inequities, we can begin to understand the relationship between the individual and the larger society. However, what is important here is how those not in positions of power adhere to or challenge the systems. As the oft-repeated phrase from Marx aptly notes, "[I]ndividuals make their own history, but not under circumstances of their own choosing."

At the uppermost level of analysis, and the first element of social reproduction theory, is the social structure, comprised of institutions and organizations that produce and distribute the dominant culture—in this case, a racial ideology that promotes the interests of the dominant group, whites. As Michael Omi and Howard Winant state, "[T]he major institutions and social relationships of U.S. society—law, political organizations, economic relationships, religion, cultural life, residential patterns, etc.—have been structured from the beginning by the racial order" (1994:79). As such, institutions (i.e., religion, the economy, education, and media), organizations, and various social relationships promote a racial ideology that supports this racial order—valuing whiteness and devaluing "nonwhiteness."

The United States is structured along racial lines, such that economic, political, social, and psychological rewards are allocated differently, based on an individual's race (Bonilla-Silva 1996, 2001). This racialized social system makes the "color line"—and the corresponding notions of superiority and inferiority—the fundamental dividing line in society. Additionally, as explained by Omi and Winant (1994), this racialized social system makes persistent the ideas that the term "American" equates with whiteness, with all groups not white characterized as "other," and that racism itself does not even exist (color-blind racism). Those in the dominant group (whites) must consistently reinforce these ideas to maintain the racialized system. For the status quo to maintain its hold, those who do not think racially must be taught to do so. One way those in power do this is through culture and ideology.

The second key element of social reproduction theory is the analysis of culture. As Henry Giroux correctly recognized, it is our social institutions that "rather than impose docility and oppression, reproduce existing power relations subtly via the production and distribution of a dominant culture" (1983:87). In the United States, social control and the maintenance of the socioeconomic system occur not through dictatorships and military force, but through the promotion and reproduction of the dominant ideas of success and mobility (Gramsci 1999/1971). The consistent maxim both native-born Americans and immigrants hear is, "If you work hard enough, you, too, can make it." All institutions, not just educational institutions, promote the ideas of the dominant class, simultaneously ensuring that their interests are met and their status not challenged. For example, the media plays a strong role in supporting the dominant ideologies of social mobility and individualism. We are encouraged to define our success based on our possessions; and if one needs help from the government or other sources, that individual is defined a failure. Part of the power of this dominant culture is that these interests are seen by the oppressor and the oppressed as not only acceptable, but as natural and rational. What this essentially does is keep people working hard to achieve a goal that many will never reach, ensuring the reproduction of the system.

In my work, I saw these first two elements—social structure and culture—working together and intersecting. Therefore, for my model of racial reproduction, I chose to integrate the two, analyzing the role of structure in terms of institutions, organizations, and segregation, alongside the cultural resources used within these systems.

The third element to understanding social reproduction is the concept of "habitus" (Bourdieu 1990a). Habitus prepares individuals to think and act a certain way based on the objective, external world and is "composed of the attitudes, beliefs, and experiences of those inhabiting one's social world" (MacLeod 1995:15). It is made up of all the individual has encountered, including his or her own experiences, the experiences of those around the individual, the interactions the individual has with others, and, importantly, what the individual receives from the culture and social structure. It is through the habitus that we see the individual not as a passive recipient of all that the dominant group imparts, but as an active agent, interpreting, challenging, resisting, and/or accepting the dominant ideologies.

While the usefulness of social reproduction theory for understanding social inequality is evident from the above analysis, what is also apparent is the overwhelming and singular use of class inequality to explain social reproduction. Consistently, theorists who have examined social reproduction, such as Samuel Bowles and Herbert Gintis (1976), Paul Willis (1978), Giroux (1983), Pierre Bourdieu (1977, 1984), and, more recently, Jay MacLeod (1995), have only applied a class inequality analysis to the social reproduction framework. While social reproduction theory is useful in helping us understand how the class structure is maintained, it ignores other very crucial elements of our social structure: specifically, racial inequality and gender inequality.[1] While I am not claiming that an analysis of racial inequality should replace that of class in social reproduction theory, in this book I attempt to incorporate race into social reproduction theory.

Racial Reproduction

Three principal elements of a racial reproduction model, along with corresponding levels of analysis, play a role in understanding racial reproduction: (1) social structure, (2) culture, and (3) habitus, or individual expressions. The racial social structure translates into a society structured along racial lines, resulting in a racial order that provides privileges and benefits to those in the advantageous racial positions (whites) and relatively few rewards to those in the subordinate positions (all others). By promoting and expressing this racial hierarchy, society's social institutions ensure the reproduction of the racial system and racism. The culture, and the ideology maintaining it, provides individuals with racial knowledge about this racial order and with conceptual and perceptual frameworks about the racialized society. Finally, individuals within this racial social structure learn from this culture and respond to these systems based on their own socially shared experiences as autonomous beings and members of racialized groups. This creates a racial habitus that provides them with commonsense notions about race, the racial hierarchy, and the racial social structure. In this manner, immigrants develop a new racial habitus that leads them to create new racial identities. It is the combination of the racial habitus and the new immigrants' racial identities that, in turn, leads immigrants to help re-create the very system they have entered and acquired. This is racial reproduction.

This process is not unique to the current wave of immigrants. To paraphrase Malcolm X, immigrants of the early 1900s quickly learned where black Americans were placed in this new society (Malcolm X 1992/1965). I am arguing here that new immigrants are also "learning race." These more recent immigrants have a unique position in our current society. Not only are they entering a "new world"—one with different racial ideas than those of the world that immigrants entered at the turn of the last century—but they are also entering a more diverse, culturally expressive society. No longer is the racial "choice" a binary one of black or white. Racial identities now are more ambiguous and fluid. Nonetheless, immigrants entering the United States today do not enter a society free of prejudices and discriminations. Instead, they enter a world where the "raceless" are the ones at the top of the social status ladder, and those either choosing to hold onto their racial minority status or forced to do so are relegated to the lower rungs. A racial ideology exists in the United States. And in much the same way as a hundred years ago, this racial ideology is one of discrimination against black Americans, in particular, as well as against all those deemed "nonwhite."

Before exploring this ideology in more detail, I define various terms used in this book, review my methods of research, and outline the book's format.

Key Terms and Methods

Race and Ethnicity

"Race" is a term used freely throughout this book. It is important at this point, though, to make clear that I am referring to *the idea of race as a social construction*. Race is a concept created, maintained, and reproduced by society. This means that race is not a natural attribute, but a socially and historically constructed one. Additionally, race is a phenomenon whose meaning is contested throughout social life, as shown, for example, by the various ways the US Census Bureau has asked about race at different times (Omi and Winant 1994). For example, the Office of Management and Budget argues that Hispanics are not a racial category and that that is why the census survey does not provide "Latino/Hispanic" as an option under the race categories. Nonetheless, many Latinos do consider themselves as belonging to a racial group. Finally, race is a component of collective identities and social structures; racial concepts were built into the fabric and foundation of our country. Therefore, by saying that race is a social construct, I am most certainly *not* saying that race is a false notion.

Native-born Americans tend to conflate race and ethnic categories. Outside academia, race is often understood as beginning and ending with skin color (George 1997). Or, as Ian Haney Lopez succinctly states, "Race may be America's single most confounding problem, but the confounding problem of race is that few people seem to know what race is" (1999:165). While social scientists still struggle to define the distinction between "race" and "ethnicity," for the lay person, the difference can be even more confusing.

Definitions of ethnicity are as ambiguous and conflicting as those of race. Essentially, for our purposes, we can conceive of an ethnic group as a collective group within the larger society, having real or assumed common ancestry and memories of a shared historical past (Schaefer 2005). Ethnicity can be based on such common issues as geographical concentration (French Canadians in Quebec), religious affiliation (Jews), or shared language (Latino/as).

For my purposes here, I conceive of race in the United States in the common-parlance sense; there are non-Hispanic whites (European-Americans), non-Hispanic blacks (African-Americans), Asians, Hispanics/Latinos, and American Indians. Because my focus in this book is on the reproduction of racism, I am primarily concerned with how these races are perceived and placed on the racial hierarchy, as well as how each group—often fluid and nondistinct—defines itself. Because race and ethnicity are often conflated terms, for both native born and newcomers, African-American means "black," and vice versa. However, because my concern is with the use of racial ideology and the reproduction of racism, I will primarily use the racial terms "black" and "white."

Ethnicity and race are among the most common categories that individuals use to organize their ideas about who they are, to evaluate their experiences and behaviors, and to understand the world around them. Ethnicity and race have to do with fundamental group processes—how we see ourselves, how we see others, and how we act on these perceptions. However, race is about power, ethnicity is not. Race is about inequality, ethnicity is not. Immigrants are not simply viewing a hierarchy of professional, middle-, and upper-class Americans at the top and lower-class, disadvantaged individuals at the bottom; they are viewing them with a "race lens": whites at the top, blacks and other racial minorities at the bottom.

Modern Racism

Modern racism is essentially about the mythic belief that everyone in the United States is treated equally regardless of race. Further, there is resistance to any meaningful actions to provide for this equality. Another belief dominates, as well: that those who have not succeeded in US society, racial minorities in particular, are where they are because of their own negative cultural characteristics.

This concept of modern racism is a combination of other, recent theories on racism as it exists currently in the United States. Combining the theoretical discussions of symbolic racism, laissez-faire racism, and color-blind racism, we can arrive at this all-encompassing construct of modern racism (Bobo, Kluegel, and Smith 1997, Hughes 1998, Bonilla-Silva 2003, Gallagher 2003, 2006). Chapters 4 and 5 further explore this construct.

Methods in Brief

Although I discuss the methods I used to obtain my information in the appendixes of this book, they are worth briefly summarizing here. I use a great deal of quotes throughout this book, collected through a variety of methods. Initially, I spent a considerable amount of time observing English-language classes at several literacy centers in a medium-sized city. After about six months of observation, I began to conduct interviews (and held one focus group) with immigrants who used the centers and individuals who worked at these centers, as well as others who worked at immigrant-service centers. Additionally, through contacts made with the immigrants there and at other services, I conducted additional individual immigrant interviews.[2] Finally, I used content analysis to examine the resources used by the various literacy centers, as well as the main local public library, which continues to maintain a prominent role in the Americanization process. Therefore, all the quotes used throughout this book were obtained for use in this research.

I strongly believe the use of qualitative interview material is the best way to research the questions I have. Because the subject of my research is both controversial and sensitive, it is likely that survey questions would not fully engage the subject enough to get rich, more complete information. By continuously probing and asking for clarifications, I can be as assured as possible that I am accurately representing my subjects. Additionally, as previously mentioned, the majority of social reproduction literature focuses on quantitative research; therefore, my work here adds a qualitative dimension to the reproduction field.

Acquiring the Dominant Ideology

Institutions and Cultural Agents

My research indicates that native-born Americans play a critical role in the incorporation process of new immigrants. While the agents of various immigrant-service institutions are certainly not the only native-born Americans that immigrants come into contact with, for immigrants with limited English-language skills, these agents may be the only native-born Americans with whom the new arrivals feel comfortable. Both the institutions and the cultural agents within these institutions reproduce the dominant and mainstream race relations ideology.

> MARTHA (native-born white American): Almost all of them [Russian and Ukrainian immigrants] are living on SSI in a poverty existence but to them, these are some of the best years of their lives. They are able to live well relative to their previous life and even some of them send money home to family and/or friends.

Martha is the director of one of the literacy centers I frequented; affiliated with the larger literacy center in "Eastern City," it is located in a national nonprofit agency and primarily serves Eastern European immigrants. For Martha, the Eastern European immigrants she sees are excellent examples of the meritocracy we live in, where hard work pays off and life here is full of opportunities and rewards.

Martha is an example of an "agent of an immigrant-service organization." These agents are often the first, and at times the only, source of knowledge about the United States the immigrant receives from a native-born US citizen. The overwhelming feeling among these agents was that immigrants work hard and that there are no barriers to their success in this country. While the immigrant may be receiving messages from their family and friends in the United States about who lives where, whom to trust and whom to avoid, and, thereby, learning the racial hierarchy, these agents are promoting modern racism: the idea that race no longer matters in the United States, that African-Americans and other racial minorities who have not succeeded have only themselves to blame, and that the government should play no role in alleviating a racism that no longer exists.

Aside from learning modern racism from these native-born citizens, immigrants acquire racial knowledge by witnessing the racial segregation so clearly evident in all institutions in the United States. For immigrants, one of the first places this occurs is in neighborhoods around the city, including their own. Immigrants also witness this in the various immigrant-services organizations they encounter; in this case, primarily the literacy centers where they come not only to learn English, but to find jobs, make friends, and "become Americans." The most evident component of this racial segregation is that those in positions of power tend to be white Americans. The immigrants I spoke with recognized this and firmly believed that those whites in power were there solely as a result of their own hard work; i.e., more evidence of meritocracy.

Therefore, not only are the agents of the various immigrant-services organizations verbally reinforcing the "American" values of meritocracy, their very presence in positions of power further reinforces this idea. Immigrants come here searching for the American Dream; they learn from the services they use that there are no obstacles to this dream, that they—and anyone in this society—can achieve this dream as long as they work hard.

Developing and Expressing a Racial Habitus

After immigrants are exposed to the racial hierarchy and segregation existent in the United States, as well as to the dominant racial ideology as expressed by native-born Americans, we begin to see this racial ideology being expressed by immigrants themselves. By expressing the dominant racial ideology, modern racism, immigrants are creating their own racial habitus. We see this happening regardless of what socioeconomic situation the immigrants find themselves in, such as with Fernando:

> FERNANDO (Peruvian): When I first came, I happened to train with the, all blacks, they were very dedicated, they were hardworking people, but then the next generation came and it was completely the opposite. Completely the opposite. When I was training . . . I have to hire some of them, well, probably about six or seven times, I have people trying to collect unemployment, one was white, the other ones were black. The problem was that they would work, they know how far, how many days or how many months, they have to work before they become eligible for unemployment, the next day, the very next day, you don't see them. They want, they always show up late, the ones that show up, I would say drunk, they want to borrow money in between, before paycheck, but then, if you want to fire them, they gonna destroy your car, they gonna destroy your [things] . . .

Fernando, a middle-class Peruvian, was typical of many of the immigrants I spoke to, regardless of their class standing. Because they came here to make a better life for themselves, they often rely on various mechanisms to explain the position of black Americans in the United States. This is only one element to learning the dominant ideology. This combination of their own experiences and beliefs, as well as what others have relayed to them from the latters' own experiences, comprise a racial habitus. This habitus does not develop in a vacuum but, instead, is a response to the larger social structure and culture the immigrant has been exposed to and witnessed. As Pierre Bourdieu has explained, the term habitus is all the socially acquired experiences that shape an individual's understanding of the "rules of the game" (Bourdieu 1990). In this case, the "game" is the racial society into which immigrants enter. They must navigate this world, learning how race is understood, what it means in the United States, what group is considered the dominant racial category and why, and where they themselves fit in.

What I learned from my research was that to construct this racial habitus, immigrants combine their home country knowledge of life in the United States with the knowledge they receive once they arrive here, from both their own compatriots and the "representatives" of US life they meet, and the cultural resources to which they are exposed. This habitus leads them to express a racial ideology consistent with that of native-born white Americans.

The particular form of racial ideology I saw expressed by immigrants was modern racism. Time and again, they echoed the kind of native-born white American expressions of modern racism others have identified (Bobo et al. 1998, Hughes 1998, Bonilla-Silva 2003, Gallagher 2003, 2006). For example, I saw many stereotypical images of blacks, with the immigrants making assumptions about motivation, activities, and work ethics.

> MANNY (Peruvian): Black people are discriminated against in this country because they have a different attitude. They have a different way of acting, of behaving. They're uneducated. They believe they have the right to everything before we [Hispanics] do. . . . Black people inside themselves, in their subconscious, they feel that they are being prejudiced against by anyone looking at them.

The immigrants professed a strong sense of the belief in meritocracy, laying claim to the idea that all that is needed in the United States is a strong work ethic and then success is assured. Further, they often expressed the idea that native-born blacks feel entitled:

> HILDA (Ecuadoran): Well, the African-Americans, of course, they feel that this is their home, they are better, they have the rights before anybody else, and yes, they do, they do look down on Latinos. {*Why do you think this?*} Well, because they feel that [Latinos] have come to this country to raid, so to speak, their territory.

This combination of accepting native-born white Americans as the legitimate power holders in the United States, believing strongly in an American meritocracy, and adopting the racial ideology of modern racism all contribute to creating a racial habitus for these new members of American society. This racial habitus, ironically, helps these newcomers become American more easily than native-born Americans, or even the immigrants themselves, realize.

Relationship Between Ideology and Identity

Learning the modern racial ideology is only one piece to the immigrants' racial habitus; this ideology also informs their own identity and their understanding of the identities of others, which further contributes to their racial habitus. By exploring how immigrants identity both their own group and other groups, we can get a sense of how they further view race in the United States.

> LISA (Colombian): *{So you think the term Hispanic should be a racial category?}* No, not a racial category, because for me race refers to white or black. *{Based on that, then, what is your race?}* I think it is white because black is not . . . *{Black does not define you?}* No.

> MANNY (Peruvian): *{Do you believe there is any benefit in describing yourself as white?}* I don't think it is a matter of how you define yourself because it is very easy to see that you are not white. It would make no sense to define myself as white, because I am not white.

> PAULA (Jamaican): *{How do you think people will see your son when he's older?}* He's not African-American so they better not call him that, but I don't know what he'll be.

Previous groups of immigrants came to the United States and quickly recognized the benefits in identifying with being white. As they rose through the ranks to middle-class status, Southern and Eastern European immigrants eventually attained this white-American status. Current waves of immigrants, largely from Central and South America and Asia, do not necessarily have, nor want, this option of white racial status. Facing struggles similar to the government strug-

gles of choosing appropriate classification schemas for racial categories in the United States, the majority of current immigrants try to
understand where they fit in the racial classifications. One aspect to
this attempt is that many of the immigrants I spoke to desire to become
American, yet simultaneously seem to believe that only whites are true
Americans.

It is in their expressions of modern racism and in the way they conceive of their own identity that new immigrants are helping to both
reproduce racism and challenge racial constructs. While fully engaging
in the American Dream and modern-racism ideologies, and accepting
the racial segregation evident in the United States as simply being consistent with this notion of meritocracy, immigrants are helping to reproduce race. However, by not believing that white and black are the only
racial category options available to them, and that they can, and potentially will, achieve a hyphenated status, immigrants are also challenging
many of our accepted racial constructs.

Finally, before detailing the format of the rest of the book, I outline
here the recent demographic changes we have seen with regard to immigration to the United States. As I said previously, earlier cohorts of
immigrants also learned the racial context and ideology of their time;
however, this current wave of immigrants, as we will see below, is a
much more diverse group than has ever previously immigrated to the
United States.

Recent Demographic Changes

According to data collected in the Current Population Survey used by
the US Census Bureau, the estimated foreign-born population of the
United States in the year 2000 was 28.4 million (see Table 1.1). This
represents an increase of 8.6 million, or 44 percent, since the 1990 census. This figure of 28.4 million individuals means that 10 percent of the
US population was foreign-born in 2000, the highest rate since 1930. In
2000, 14.5 million (50 percent) of the foreign-born residents were from
Latin America and 7.2 million were from Asia (26 percent of the foreign-born population). Those from Latin America include approximately
27 percent from Mexico, about 10 percent from the Caribbean, and
about 7 percent each from Central America and South America. Only
4.4 million, or 15 percent, of foreign-born residents in 2000 were
European-born. This small percentage is significantly different from that

Table 1.1   Immigrants to the United States by Decades/Peak Periods of Immigration

Year	Foreign-Born Population	Percentage of US Population
1870	5.6 million	14
1890	9.2 million	15
1910	13.5 million	15
1970	9.6 million	5
1980	14.1 million	6
1990	19.8 million	8
2000	28.4 million	10

in 1970, when the majority (62 percent) listed a European country as their place of birth (2000 US Census).

Finally, approximately 8.1 percent of the foreign-born are from other regions, such as Africa. These numbers are significant in terms of the demographic characteristics of the US population; importantly, the numbers indicate that a higher percentage of the foreign-born population is "nonwhite" than ever before (see Tables 1.2 and 1.3).

Format of the Book

The next chapter begins to implement the model of racial reproduction based on the data I collected through interviews and field work. As mentioned previously, the first stage of the process of racial reproduction is immigrants' efforts to understand what the racial social structure is; I

Table 1.2   Foreign-born Population by Region of Birth

Year	Country of Origin			
	Europe	Latin America	Asia	Other Regions
1970	5.7 million	1.8 million	.8 million	.4 million
1980	5.1 million	4.4 million	2.5 million	1.2 million
1990	4.4 million	8.4 million	5.0 million	1.3 million
2000	4.4 million	14.5 million	7.2 million	1.6 million

Table 1.3   Foreign-born Percentage by Region of Birth

	Country of Origin			
Year	Europe	Latin America	Asia	Other Regions
1970	62%	19%	9%	1%
1980	39%	33%	19%	2%
1990	23%	44%	26%	2.5%
2000	15%	51%	25.5%	6%

here discuss how immigrants become aware of this structure and from whom they receive this knowledge. In this way, I look generally at the current racial social structure in the United States, and the corresponding racial ideology, and provide a more developed definition of modern racism. Additionally, I go into greater detail about the assimilation process and how it has differed for immigrant groups at various points in history.

Chapter 3 takes a step back and explores some of the ways immigrants think about the United States before their immigration process. These preconceptions can provide insight into what immigrants bring with them in terms of their knowledge of race and the racial hierarchy in the United States. Further, this chapter examines some of the ways immigrants perceive of race in their home countries, providing us with a context for their understanding of race in the United States.

The next step in immigrants' knowledge of racial ideology in the United States occurs when immigrants come into contact with the racial hierarchy in this country, including within the immigrant-services organizations they frequent. This examination, in Chapter 4, includes an analysis of the cultural resources used by these organizations to impart "American ideas." Finally, by looking at the agents within these organizations, we can begin to see some of the more overt ways immigrants learn the current racial beliefs. These agents play an important role in sustaining the racial structure and hierarchy; it is through them that immigrants are more fully exposed to the dominant ideology.

Chapter 5 explores the expression of this racial knowledge. I further explain the ideas of a racial habitus, as well as the related idea of racialization, and we see the full expressions of modern racism as articulated by the immigrants I interviewed. I discuss what I term a "racialized worldview" and "race talk," where these immigrants begin to give us a sense of how they view race and race relations in the United States. In particular, I break down the components of modern racism, as expressed by those interviewed, and examine how they believe in the American Dream ideology, in the minimization of racism, and in cultural racism, as uttered through common stereotypes. It is in this chapter that we begin to understand how racial inequality is reproduced by new members of society on a daily basis.

Chapter 6 revisits the ideas of assimilation theory discussed in Chapter 2, and also explores how part of this assimilation process is acquiring a racialized identity consistent with the adoption of a modern racism ideology. I explore how these views of race help to inform the immigrant racial identity, looking at how the respondent immigrants perceive themselves in relation to others (and how they believe others view them) and also at their ideas and visions concerning their future group identity.

Finally, Chapter 7 looks at ways we might begin to challenge this reproduction process. I examine some interracial tensions, and briefly discuss multiracial coalitions and the possibilities for educators, policy makers, and others to help stop the enduring legacy of racism.

Notes

1. In this book I will only be focusing on the aspect of racial inequality and will not discuss gender inequality and reproduction. However, for an excellent discussion of the intersections of race and gender, see Philomena Essed (1991) and Patricia Hill Collins (2000).

2. I benefited from the services of an assistant from Puerto Rico who conducted several of the interviews in Spanish with those who had limited English language abilities.

2

The Racial Structure of US Society

FOR US TO UNDERSTAND THE SOCIAL structure immigrants enter, we must fully understand what they are witnessing and learning. Thus, we begin with a brief discussion of the racial social structure and racial segregation existing in the United States, including a description of the demographics in the region and city in which I conducted my research. Next, we explore the racial ideology and assimilation processes for immigrants during the last great migration (1890–1924) and compare them to the racial ideologies and assimilation processes prevalent for the current wave of immigrants, with an examination of such current ideologies as laissez-faire racism, symbolic racism, color-blind racism, and racial apathy. For the purposes of this book, these racial ideologies can be collapsed into a succinct category of "modern racism." Finally, this chapter examines the various racial classifications that, scholars maintain, exist today. Whether one considers the white-black divide propounded during the last century, the black-nonblack racial divide argued more recently, or the tri- or multiracial classifications put forth by others, immigrants are still entering an environment in which whites maintain their position at the top and black Americans are consistently pushed into a position at the bottom. Only by fully comprehending the constructs that immigrants are entering into can we begin to make sense of what constructs they are acquiring.

Racialized Social System

A racial hierarchy in the United States places some (whites) in a superior social status position and all others in a lower position. The structure, therefore, is divided according to socially constructed racial categories, with some individuals receiving rewards and privileges because of their higher-status positions. This system of differential rewards and privileges based on race is not a new development in the United States; from its inception, the United States has been a racial and racist society. Early European settlers used racist practices and beliefs to justify the genocide of Native Americans because of their "inferior" cultural characteristics, to implement the slave trade, and to deny African-Americans full citizenship. US lawmakers continued these practices after the revolution and the civil war, passing immigration laws that privileged those deemed white and applying discriminatory and separatist Jim Crow laws. Currently, racism in the United States expresses itself in less overt ways and in a more institutionalized manner. Our welfare policies and system (Neubeck and Cazenave 2001), our de facto segregation in cities and schools (Kozol 1991, Massey and Denton 1993), our unequal punishments and sentences within the criminal justice system (Cole 1999), our segregated religious organizations—all work together to create a racial social structure in the United States that benefits those deemed white. The foundations of the state—including the economy, educational system, and media—support and reinforce this racist and racial system.

The US economic system continues to oppress and exploit racial minorities and, more specifically, black Americans. Slavery established the position of black Americans on the bottom of the economic structure; after slavery, the system of sharecropping further reinforced this status. The great migration of former slaves from the South to the North reproduced economic competition between blacks and poor whites, enabling white capitalists to pit the two groups against each other. Since that time, the combination of persistent wealth disparities, economic downturns, and discriminatory housing, lending, and employment practices have continued to adversely affect black Americans as well as other racial minority groups.

This economic structure is supported by a racist political structure that continues to privilege whites over all others. The state maintained the Europeans' racist policies by supporting slavery and then by allowing the South to establish Jim Crow laws following the civil war. The US Constitution originally provided citizenship only to those deemed white; Congress and the Supreme Court have attempted, with more or less success over the years, to limit citizenship (or "white status") to those perceived as superior. Immigration laws, marriage laws, and voting rights have consistently been based on racial criteria—adjusted depending on who fit (or fits) the dominant white standards for acceptance. Racist government policies, established since the beginning of US history, have created, produced, and maintained racial differences and differential rewards based on racial differences (Haney Lopez 1996, Omi and Winant 1994).

Our other major institutions have also historically been structured along racial and racist lines. The school systems, at one time segregated by law, are, de facto, now even more segregated. As Jonathan Kozol points out, in New York state seven out of eight black and Latino children go to segregated schools (2006). Our media has also consistently contributed to the dominant ideologies of racism in this country; moreover, above all other institutions, the media has the largest impact on individuals around the world. Before immigrating to the United States, immigrants often come into contact with such US media sources as films, television, radio, magazines, and newspapers. Globalization and the media's worldwide market have helped expose individuals worldwide to the racist and stereotyped images of minorities in general and of black Americans more specifically (Suarez-Orozco and Suarez-Orozco 2001). The implications of this institutionalized racism are that all members of US society view this racial hierarchy and, using the current racial ideology, justify it (Wilson 1996).

This macro view of the US racial social structure is replicated on a smaller level as well. In cities around the country, groups are segregated based on race, with white elites continuing to hold power in most major institutions and organizations. The region in which I conducted my research is no exception.

Location of This Study

Region

My study was conducted in the Northeast, where 22.6 percent of the total US foreign-born population resides. (Conversely, 12.3 percent of the population in the Northeast is foreign-born.) The foreign-born demographics differ depending on the region of the United States and proximity to foreign countries. For example, the greatest percentage of Mexican immigrants is in the West, as is the greatest percentage of Asian immigrants. In the Northeast, the greatest concentration of immigrants is Latin American, with 43.4 percent of its foreign-born population being from that part of the world. Of the total US Latin American foreign-born population, those from South America and the Caribbean are concentrated in the Northeast (45.5 percent of South American immigrants and 46 percent of Caribbean immigrants live in the Northeast).

Eastern City[1]

The city I chose as a model for my research ("Eastern City") is centrally located in a state where 8.7 percent of the population is foreign-born and 18.3 percent of the population claims to speak a language other than English in the home. The demographics of this population reflect the larger Northeast area, and are largely reflected in my respondents. Essentially, the majority of my respondents are from Latin America (specifically, Central and South America) and the Caribbean (see Appendix B for the list of my respondents).

Regardless of where they first immigrated to, all the immigrants in my study chose to make Eastern City their home. Therefore, they were not necessarily cognizant of the racial social structure of the larger country, but were influenced and affected by the racial social structure of the city in which they resided. Because of this, it is necessary to look at some of the basic demographics of this city.

The majority of my respondents lived within the city limits of Eastern City. According to the 2000 US Census, there are approximately 48,000 whites, 47,000 blacks, and 50,000 Hispanics living in Eastern City. However, if we include the surrounding suburbs (Eastern County), we count an additional 680,200 whites, 33,000 blacks, and 50,000 Hispanics. These numbers provide insight into the predominance of whites living in the suburbs of Eastern City, a reflection of the segregation existent around the country. When we look more specifically at areas within Eastern City, we see segregation among neighborhoods as well. For example, there is one area in Eastern City that is predominantly black American; in this area, 24 percent of the population is white and 56 percent of the population is black. Across town, however, there is an area where 64 percent of the population is Latino and 36 percent is white.

The census also tells us that there are approximately 100,700 foreign-born living in Eastern County, an increase since 1990, when there were approximately 85,000 foreign-born. Also since 1990, according to the census, both white and black populations decreased in Eastern County, while the number of Hispanics increased by almost 40,000 individuals.

Racial segregation within cities is a reflection of a combination of factors. The majority of immigrants I spoke with were increasingly likely to be living with either native-born black Americans (the West Indians, in particular), or native-born or foreign-born Hispanics. Black/white residential segregation is directly related to a history of housing and lending discrimination on the part of whites (Massey and Denton 1993). Persistent antiblack attitudes fuel residential segregation, leading to poor black communities highly segregated from the rest of society. Newcomers see this segregation and attempt to distance themselves emotionally from it (Zubrinsky and Bobo 1996). Often they claim that their housing situation is temporary and that they intend to move "up" as soon as possible.

This institutionalized racism, in all its variant forms, is only able to exist because of entrenched racial ideology. Just as the institutionalized forms of oppression have changed to conform to the historical context, the racial ideology has changed as well.

Immigrants and the Racial Context: Then and Now

Like immigration and institutionalized racism, racial ideology is both a social and a historical process. Furthermore, it changes according to the currently acceptable belief system. In the early 1900s, it was both common and acceptable for whites to be explicitly racist. By exploring the racial ideology at this time, along with the process of "becoming white" experienced by the majority of earlier immigrants, we can observe racial reproduction in a historical context.

Immigration and Racial Ideology at the Turn of the Twentieth Century

By the late 1800s, the scientific community had largely rejected most of the biological explanations for race. Instead, new concepts of race, and fresh justifications for beliefs in racial inferiority and superiority, arose from the misappropriation of the works of Spencer and Darwin. Ostensibly deriving from Spencer's ideas of "survival of the fittest" and Darwin's ideas of natural selection, Social Darwinism argued that races are at different stages on an evolutionary scale. This theory continued to justify the position of the white race at the top of the racial hierarchy. The eugenics movement developed out of these concepts of Social Darwinism, essentially positing that intelligence comes from superior human stock and that characteristic traits are inherited as well, with proof of both of these contentions found in race differences.

As immigration steadily increased, the white Anglo-Saxon Protestant elite became concerned not only that immigrants were unable to assimilate, but also that they came from "inferior racial stock." Racism toward Irish, African-Americans, and Native Americans quickly developed into a larger pattern of racism toward all "other," particularly as immigration of Southern and Eastern Europeans reached a peak toward the turn of the twentieth century. Fear of a seemingly unassimilable population increased white racist beliefs, which in turn became institutionalized through the use of immigration laws and quotas as well as through policies of segregation in housing, employment, and education (Haney Lopez 1996).

The belief, as Karen Brodkin Sacks explains, that "real Americans were white and real whites came from northwest Europe" (1998:81) is exemplified in the immigrant policies and quotas first set for the Chinese in 1882, and then again in 1924 for Southern and Eastern Europeans by the National Origins Quota Act of 1927. Under this act, the percentage of visas was based on the last names of US citizens from the 1890 US Census; thus, 82 percent of the visas were allocated to Northern and Western Europeans and 16 percent to Southern and Eastern Europeans; the remaining 2 percent went to immigrants from virtually the rest of the world—with Asian immigrants still excluded. Because so few Northern and Western Europeans had been entering the country compared to Southern and Eastern Europeans, a majority of the visas went unused. This belief in the superiority of whiteness resulted in much of the anti-immigrant rhetoric during the early 1900s in the United States.

Throughout the 1910s, 1920s, and 1930s, laws, customs, and institutions privileged whiteness and persons deemed "white." Practices by the state, the economy, the media, education, and other US institutions promoted white dominance and a white racist culture that denigrated any deviation from whiteness. These practices established and maintained what W.E.B. DuBois termed the "color line" as the fundamental division in the United States. However, as opposed to the commonly portrayed binary color line dividing whites and blacks, some more accurately argue that we, in fact, have a "color hierarchy." Based on the criteria set by the dominant racial group, whites are accorded the dominant status, blacks the subordinate status, and all other racial groups are struggling and striving to move up this "racial ladder" in order to get closer to the superordinate status of whiteness (Roediger 1991, Lowe 1996, Jacobson 1998). However, still other scholars (Lee, Bean, Batalova, and Sandhu 2003, Gans 1999, Yancey 2003) argue that, rather than either a white-versus-black divide or a multiracial hierarchy, we are now entering a black-versus-nonblack divide, where black remains the sole lower-status position and all others struggle to be defined in opposition to this category.

It became clear very quickly to immigrants entering between the peak immigration years of 1880 and 1924 that to be accorded the privileges surrounding whiteness, they needed to "become white." As Ian Haney Lopez demonstrates, "Immigrants participated in the debates on naturalization, organizing civic groups around the issues of citizenship, writing in the immigrant press, and lobbying local, state, and federal governments" (1996:4), all in the hopes of attaining white status. Several authors (Brodkin Sacks 1998, Jacobson 1998, Ignatiev 1995, Roediger 1991), mostly through historical research, examine how immigrants' white racial identity development has been influenced by the racial social structure. As Matthew Jacobson notes, "The European immigrants' experience was decisively shaped by their entering an arena where Europeanness—that is to say, whiteness—was among the most important possessions one could lay claim to" (1998:8).

A consensus among these historians is that for the European immigrant, white racial inclusion was dependent on black racial exclusion. Nowhere is this more evident than with the Irish workers of the nineteenth century who fought hard to distinguish themselves from the slave labor associated with blacks. David Roediger argues that there was a public and psychological wage to whiteness for the workers in the nineteenth and twentieth centuries; as they became middle class, they continued to "whiten," and as they "whitened" they were embraced by white Protestant elites (1991).

James Barrett and Roediger (1997) maintain that becoming white and becoming American was a two-sided process for immigrants in the twentieth century; immigrants simultaneously underwent a process of racial categorizing and development of new identities. New immigrants quickly learned that the worst they could be was "colored," and their consciousness of an in-between racial status led to a desire for literal distance from nonwhites. Individuals entering the United States began to form collective group identities in opposition to those around them. Race, historically, is the effect of relations of opposition where the dialectical process of construction means that the creation of the category "the same" involves the creation of the category "the other" (Bonilla-Silva 1996). Immigrants came to see themselves in ethnic and racial categories, while simultaneously expressing the racial prejudice that accompanies this construction.

Early Theories of Racial and Ethnic Identity and Assimilation

It was within the context of overt racist ideology and white superiority that the early ideas of assimilation theory arose. During the 1920s, with proponents such as Robert Park at the University of Chicago, the idea developed that all these different cultures would come together and form one national culture: American. This process is now known as "straight-line assimilation," which Park explained in his race relations cycle, a four-stage process in which immigrants went through the first three stages—contact, accommodation, and assimilation—until they reached the final stage of amalgamation, achieved through intermarriage and reproduction (Park 1950). This process meant a transformation of individual identity, which often involved abandoning one's identification with an ethnic group. Essentially, to become white, and therefore American, meant to lose one's ethnic distinctiveness. Living with one foot in the old world and one foot in the new, the immigrant adults of that period struggled to maintain their identity as they became Americans. Many immigrants viewed this total assimilation process as the only way to achieve socioeconomic success. Nowhere was this more evident than with their children and with those who immigrated as children. For example, throughout the public school systems, the prevailing point of view was that teaching US norms, customs, and morés would create a unified nation (Berrol 1995). To pursue the American Dream, the immigrants at the turn of the last century, and especially their children, recognized they would have to shed many of their old, "ethnic" ways.

As noted earlier, at the same time that immigrants recognized the need to transform their own identities, they also came to understand how racial minorities, specifically black Americans, were treated. Immigrants worked hard to distance themselves from racial minorities; attempting to be seen as white was only the first step. Participating in racial segregation in housing, education, and employment, the immigrants of the 1880s–1920s eventually became white in both identity and racial ideology. What this did was not only produce more white Americans, but it succeeded in reproducing the systemic racism and racial hierarchy already in existence. As Joe Feagin says,

> For several centuries now, most whites not in the elites have accepted the society's racist hierarchy, along with fewer socioeconomic resources than the elites, because of their access to the privileges, opportunities, and cultural resources associated with being white and because they have bought into the ideology of racism. (2000:30)

Moving beyond Park's melting-pot theory, ethnic pluralists of the 1960s began to emerge. Resulting from the civil rights movement and the many other racial and ethnic movements of the 1960s and 1970s, such as the Chicano movement and La Raza, there emerged a pride in one's ethnic or racial group identity, which had a corresponding influence on how social scientists thought about these constructs. Along with proponents such as Nathan Glazer and Daniel P. Moynihan in their well-known book, *Beyond the Melting Pot* (1963), these theorists believed that ethnicity is neither fixed and handed down from generation to generation, nor does it disappear as individuals adapt to US society; but, instead, ethnicity emerges out of the process of adaptation to US society. The stages of this new, pluralist concept begin with the traditional traits and behaviors immigrants bring with them. These cultural characteristics do not need to disappear completely, but "must be transformed to survive" (Alba 1985:9). The next step is the merging of the old-world ways and the distinct US experience of the particular group. The final outcome is a new kind of ethnicity, one that is adaptable to each group's particular US experience and that enables its members to identify ethnically. This argument is essentially the one that W. I. Thomas and Florian Znaniecki discuss in their classic book, *The Polish Peasant in Europe and America* (1923); as they maintain, the ethnic identity that emerges is neither Polish nor American, but Polish-American. This hyphenated identity emerges from Polish traditions, new conditions of life, and US social values as the immigrant sees and interprets them.

However, because of what many see as a faulty impression of assimilation (Alba 1985), the ethnic-pluralist theory does not differ greatly from the original melting-pot theory. Those subscribing to the ethnic-pluralist view argued for the existence of an ethnicity that was actually disappearing in cultures and communities (Steinberg 1989). Other sociologists began to recognize the hollow ethnic identity that had emerged out of the assimilation and Americanization of the second-generation "white ethnics," defined by Herbert Gans as "symbolic ethnicity" (1979). Furthermore, the ethnic-pluralist interpretation continued to assert that cultural traits directly affected socioeconomic status, essentially blaming the victim for the group's position in society and ignoring the role of structural constraints on social mobility.

Both the melting-pot and the ethnic pluralist theories were only useful as long as the majority of immigrants came from European countries. Immigrants from Southern and Eastern Europe were seen initially as an inferior race, unwanted by the dominant white Anglo-Saxons in power. Eventually, by adopting a hyphenated American identity, by assimilating

American cultural values—including the current racial ideologies which placed black Americans on the bottom of the racial hierarchy—these immigrants helped to reproduce the racial social system into which they had entered. During the peak immigration period from 1880 to 1924, immigrants arrived primarily from Southern and Eastern European countries. Immigrants today are primarily from Central and South America, West Indies, and Asia (see Tables 1.1, 1.2, and 1.3 in Chapter 1) and therefore may never be seen as white. The questions then become, what does this mean for their assimilation process, and how does this process work with regard to the current racial ideology?

Changing Racial Ideologies

Throughout the 1950s, 1960s, and 1970s, ideas about the essentialism of race and the racist practices of the local, state, and federal governments, as well as small businesses and large corporations, were challenged by black Americans and white liberal sympathizers. The civil rights movement challenged overt racism, such as that expressed by Social Darwinists and the eugenics movement, and it became no longer acceptable by the general public. Instead, by the late 1970s and 1980s, new forms of racism began to emerge: symbolic racism, laissez-faire racism, and, eventually, color-blind racism. The civil rights movement had forced the federal government to take action and institutionalize such racial reforms as affirmative action. As Michael Omi and Howard Winant (1994) state, the black movements of the 1960s fundamentally changed the meaning of racial identity and of race itself.

For a brief period of time, the civil rights movement established a new dominant ideology: that black Americans had been unfairly treated and deserved some restitution for the injustices done to them and that any overtly racist policies needed to be repealed. This shift affected not only black Americans, but also the openly racist immigration policies that had been implemented in the 1920s. Coming out of World War II and witnessing the eugenics-inspired Holocaust, policymakers felt compelled to alter the clearly racist immigration laws of the 1920s, which heavily favored those from western and northern European countries. The quotas were lifted; the Immigration Reform Act of 1965 established relatively open immigration policies, which had a profound effect on increasing Asian and Latino immigration. This fundamentally (and literally) changed the face of immigration, from one dominated by European immigrants to one dominated by those from various Asian and Latin American countries. Meanwhile, although there continued to be positive changes among whites in their beliefs about racial minority groups, whites in the late 1970s began to demonstrate various forms of a more covert racism.

Current Racial Ideologies

One of the earlier terms to define this new kind of racism was what some called "symbolic racism" (Henry and Sears 2002, Kinder and Sears 1981, McConahay and Hough 1976). Essentially, researchers surveying whites found that they tended to reject overtly blatant antiblack attitudes while simultaneously expressing intolerant feelings about such policies as busing or affirmative action (Bobo 1988). As Michael Hughes explains, "[S]ymbolic racism represents the belief by whites that blacks violate traditional US values and thus do not deserve any special help" (1998:45). Believing that racial discrimination had been addressed and repaired, whites now began to resent any special treatment they perceived blacks receiving from the government.

However, some scholars began to challenge this idea of symbolic racism; they maintained that by using the term "symbolic," researchers were ignoring the rational objections that whites had to what they saw as intrusions on their way of life (Bobo 2004). These scholars argued that whites were responding to social policies (like busing) as a threat to their social world and social status location. Calling this form of racism they identified as "laissez-faire racism," they argued it was about whites recognizing and wanting to maintain their superior status (Bobo, Kluegel, and Smith 1997, Bobo 2004). Steven Tuch and Jack Martin define laissez-faire racism as "an ideology that attributes black disadvantages to supposed characteristics of blacks themselves, such as lack of attachment to the work ethic, and denies the potency of structural determinants of conditions in black communities" (1998:3). These theorists propose that there is a sense among whites that they work for what they have; that blacks themselves are to be blamed for their lower socioeconomic status; and that any black demands to remedy this situation are encroachments on whites' own, just rewards.

Both of these ideologies, symbolic racism and laissez-faire racism, are formed on the idea that for many whites there is overwhelming support for the principle that all people should be treated equally regardless of race or ethnic background, but that there is much less support for any policy implementation of this principle (Bobo, Kluegel, and Smith 1997).

A third form of current racial ideology can be called "racial apathy"

(Forman 2004). Enlarging on the belief that whites have an unwilling-
ness to address racially disparate treatment, researchers use this term to
express the idea that whites are not even concerned about this disparate
treatment. As Tyrone Forman explains, there are two reasons whites
would express racial apathy: either they believe that minorities are in a
low status due to their own deficiencies, or they are simply ignorant of
racial inequality.

Blaming racial minorities' status on those minorities' presumed
deficiencies and cultural differences, whites are able to practice these
various forms of current racial ideology, including the ideology of color-
blind racism. Arguing that the government has corrected the racist policies of the past, everyone has equal opportunities now, hard work can
move anyone ahead, and, importantly, that (theoretically) no one should
be treated differently because of the color of their skin, whites can claim
to be color blind (Bonilla-Silva 2003). Additionally, by citing the examples of "model minorities"—those racial minority groups who have succeeded to a certain extent in achieving social mobility—white ethnics
can comfortably claim that racism does not exist anymore and everyone
is now treated equally. While in the past Jews were often cited as the
example of a model minority group, more recently Asians have been
held up as an example of a socially mobile racial minority group.
However, as Stephen Steinberg (1989) correctly notes, for both Jews
and Asians this image has never been quite accurate. For example, currently Cambodians, the Hmong, and Laotians have some of the highest
poverty rates of all groups in the United States. Furthermore, the model
minority concept ignores the structural factors that contributed to their
supposed success.

Pulling from these diverse concepts of racial ideology, Eduardo
Bonilla-Silva (2003) developed four frames evident in color-blind
racism. First, abstract liberalism exists where both a political and economic liberalism mean that whites believe in the idea of equal opportunity, meritocracy, and individualism. Second, whites rely on naturalization
to argue that any disparities are naturally occurring phenomena. Third, a
culturally based argument exists to explain racial inequality. And, finally,
there is a minimization of overt racism, from which fact whites can claim
that racism no longer exists nor affects minorities' life chances
(2003:28). In order to benefit from the various ideological constructions
of the current forms of racism, I use the term "modern racism."
Combining the previous theories of racial ideology, this term encompasses the following ideas: (1) everyone should be, and currently is, treated
equally regardless of the color of their skin or ethnic background; (2)

there should be no policy changes or legislation to ensure this equal treatment; (3) any racial inequality that does exist is because of either natural or cultural deficiencies on the part of the lower-status group; and (4) anyone who works hard enough can move up the social status ladder.

As I argue in this book, these are the same arguments being used by immigrants entering US society. The current wave of immigrants, unable to become white, are nonetheless learning and then reproducing the dominant ideologies of modern racism; this learning process is occurring as part of their assimilation process. Various scholars have documented the very different forms of assimilation that these newer immigrants and their children are experiencing; we must recognize that, along with all the other components of US society that they are adopting, these new arrivals are also absorbing and learning modern racism.

Current Assimilation Theories

As discussed previously, extensive research (Brodkin Sacks 1998, Jacobson 1998, Barrett and Roediger 1997) informs us that for most Southern and Eastern European immigrants at the turn of the twentieth century, becoming part of the white racial-status group meant simultaneously excluding black Americans. To become not only white but American as well, immigrants at this time learned quickly that they had to reject and distance themselves from black Americans. In hoping to enter into this exclusive and desired social and racial status, these immigrants helped solidify the creation of an "other" category for all those not considered white (Bonilla-Silva 1996). This belief in their own attained superiority was critical to the racialization process.

Where does this racialization process leave the current wave of immigrants? While white immigrants—those coming from such places as England, Italy, France, and Ireland—are perhaps eventually perceived as white Americans, the majority of immigrants entering the United States in the recent past are largely considered nonwhite by the majority native-born population. If immigrants are adopting much of the same racial ideologies present in the dominant society, how, then, does this acquisition of current racial ideologies affect their identification and assimilation process?

The dramatic shift in modern immigration—with new immigrants coming to the United States not primarily from Europe but from Asia and Latin America—has led ethnicity theorists and immigration scholars to develop new theories and concepts of assimilation and adaptation, although some recent scholars continue to promote the more traditional forms of assimilation (Alba and Nee 2003, Waldinger and Feliciano 2004) by claiming essentially that the majority of immigrants and their children will eventually assimilate into the dominant culture in much the same way previous waves of immigrants did. For example, Richard Alba and Victor Nee reconfigure the mainstream assimilation theories of the past and argue that there is currently a weakening role of ethnicity. However, other scholars, discussed below, recognize that immigrant groups now—racially distinct from the dominant racial majority—do not necessarily have the same options for ethnic identity; i.e., linear assimilation, acculturation, and adaptation into the dominant social structure. Some of the same difficulties face the current first- and second-generation immigrants as faced immigrants at the turn of the twentieth century; for instance, intergenerational conflict, often centered around a child's desire to become Americanized and drop many of the parents' more traditional ways. However, new conflicts arise when the majority of current immigrants cannot become part of the dominant culture because of racism. Moreover, most immigrants entering the country currently are persons of color and are exposed to discrimination very different from the kind earlier immigrants experienced. As a result of this and other factors, some theorists, such as Alejandro Portes and Ruben Rumbaut, maintain that their process of assimilation will be very different:

> The present second generation is better defined as undergoing a process of segmented assimilation where outcomes vary across immigrant minorities and where rapid integration and acceptance into the American mainstream represent just one possible alternative. (2001: 45)

According to Portes and Rumbaut, four factors determine the path of assimilation: the history of the parent generation, the acculturation path of the parents and children, the cultural and economic barriers confronted by the second generation, and the resources available for confronting these barriers. These scholars correctly identify a major factor in the assimilation process of the second generation (and of the first as well): the reception of the host society to the newcomers. They note, "In America, race is a paramount criterion of social acceptance that can overwhelm the influence of class background, religion, or language" (2001: 47).

As a result of these varying factors, segmented-assimilation scholars (Portes and Rumbaut 2001, Portes and Zhou 1993, Jensen and Chitose 1994, Zhou and Xiong 2005, Portes, Fernandez-Kelly, and Haller 2005) argue that there are, in fact, three paths to assimilation, in contrast to the single, straight-line path touted by earlier assimilation theorists. First, there is the possibility of similar straight-line assimilation, which these scholars term "consonant acculturation." In this case, assimilation occurs at the same rate and pace for both generations, and the result is full acculturation into the dominant culture. Second, there is the possibility of "selective acculturation." Here, a strong and sizeable ethnic community enables the generations to sustain the parents' home language, culture, and traditions. Finally, and what most segmented-assimilation scholars argue is happening to the majority of immigrants and their children, is "dissonant acculturation" or downward assimilation. When this happens, the second and subsequent generations reject their parents' culture as well as the dominant culture and, instead, embrace the minority oppositional culture. Entering into a racist society and perceived as nonwhite, virtually all immigrants experience racism and discrimination. Further, they often arrive in poverty and, therefore, are likely to settle in inner-city ghetto areas. This means that for many immigrants their children are more likely to adopt the norms and attitudes of the lower-status minority culture than of the dominant, white mainstream culture. This can often mean rejecting education, joining gangs, and using and selling drugs (Portes et al. 2005). Additionally, not only does this oppositional culture affect the children's assimilation paths, but it also affects their identity.

> Children of Asian, black, mulatto, and mestizo immigrants cannot escape their ethnicity and race, as defined by the mainstream. Their enduring physical differences from whites and the equally persistent strong effects of discrimination based on those differences, especially against black persons, throws a barrier in the path of occupational mobility and social acceptance. (Portes et al. 2005:1006)

The next section explores these ideas in terms of identity and its impact on the racial social structure and hierarchy in the United States.

Racial Categories and Classification

The racial categories existent in the United States are both historical and social constructions. While much of the social characteristics come from definitions imposed upon groups by others, some of the social construction occurs from the groups' self-creation of identity. As mentioned repeatedly, immigrants are entering into a racist and racial society. However, recently, scholars have argued for a variety of ways to interpret these racial category constructions.

First, as opposed to DuBois's concept of the black-white racial divide mentioned earlier, more recent scholars (Lee et al. 2003, Gans 1999, Yancey 2003) argue that there is a black-nonblack divide, where black remains the sole lower-status position; given this divide, Asians and Latinos struggle to be defined as white. For example, using data on intermarriage rates and multiracial identification for Latinos and Asians, Jennifer Lee et al. claim that "the color line may not be as strong (or may be shifting more rapidly) for these newer immigrant groups compared to blacks" (47). Furthermore, we can particularly see how this might be the case for black immigrants, such as those from the West Indies. For these immigrants, while they may want to claim a separate ethnic identity from black Americans, their skin color often means they have little choice in this matter from the larger society.

West Indian immigrants are in the unique position of appearing to be black, with native-born Americans and even other immigrants largely ignoring their immigrant status. Philip Kasinitz (1992) suggests that before the 1980s, the relatively small number of West Indians meant that they generally identified with black Americans; however, post-1980s, he claims, ethnicity began to play an increasing role in West Indians' lives. What some researchers found is that for the West Indian immigrant, retaining immigrant identity can actually "ease economic and social incorporation into the United States" (Waters 1999:5). Mary Waters asserts that the West Indian immigrants she interviewed recognized that if they lost their immigrant status, they would become black Americans, which represented downward mobility, so they tended to distance themselves from black Americans. As she writes, "For these immigrants becoming American also entails becoming American black, which they perceive as a lower social status than staying a West Indian" (1999:93). However, through persistent and obvious racial discrimination that leads to lower wages in bad jobs and worse neighborhoods and schools, these immigrants quickly come to realize race as a master status can begin to overwhelm any other specific immigrant or ethnic identity. Recent non-white immigrants are likely to experience discrimination in everyday life, and these experiences will affect their identity-development process.

A second theory, contrasting the previous idea of a racial hierarchy where whites are on the top, blacks are on the bottom, and all others are striving to make their way up the ladder to the top, is that there are, in fact, three racial classifications into which most groups can be placed (Bonilla-Silva and Glover 2004). This tri-racial system still means whites on the top and minorities (or "collective blacks") on the bottom, but it places a category of "honorary whites" in the middle. Similar to Mia Tuan's idea of "forever foreigners" (1998), this middle category includes those from Asian and Latino backgrounds, who often find themselves pitted against black Americans in competition for jobs or housing, but are rarely able to penetrate the upper-status levels of whites, either.

Against this black-white polarization of race in the United States, the racial identity of Asians is placed in some intermediate position (Visweswaran 1997). Many Asian communities are also in the difficult position of being perceived as the "model minority" groups, with whites using them as the example against which all other racial minorities should be compared. Thus, Asians have a racially ambiguous identity, perceived as racially distinct from whites, yet not nonwhite (Kibria 1996). While simultaneously valorizing their position relative to other racial minorities, whites also perceive Asians as foreign and unable to be assimilated and, therefore, continue to stigmatize and ostracize them (Min and Kim 1999, Ong 1996).

Finally, a third theory, similar to the previous one, argues that beyond the black-white model of racial categories, a multiracial category is more widespread in the United States than ever before, largely due to the increase in Latino immigration (Rodriguez 2000).

Latinos are in a unique situation in terms of racial identity development, in that Latino immigrants run the continuum from those having very dark skin to those who look white. For example, white Cubans arrived in the United States in the 1960s, fleeing the early years of the Cuban Revolution, while in the 1980s, black Cubans arrived fleeing poverty. As Roberto Suro says,

> Latino immigrants defy basic assumptions about culture and class because they undermine the perspective that divides the nation into white and nonwhite, a perspective that is the oldest and most enduring element of America's social structure. (1998:7)

In Latin American countries, the strict US definition of race as "either black or white" is neither used nor necessarily understood. Instead, there are intermediate categories; skin color is an individual, not a group, marker, where even siblings within one family can be seen as different colors. Latinos come to the United States with their own definitions of race and their own racial hierarchies. As Clara Rodriguez writes, "For many Latinos, race is primarily cultural; multiple identities are a normal state of affairs; and 'racial mixture' is subject to many different, sometimes fluctuating, definitions" (2000:5). Entering the United States,

Latino immigrants are expected, and often forced, to choose one racial category; the US census, for example, has a limited number of racial categories from which to choose.

As clear evidence of this partial rejection of the binary categories in the United States, the 2000 US Census indicates that a significant number of Latinos, more than any other immigrant or racial/ethnic group, marked "Other" for their racial category (US Census Bureau 2000). Numerous scholars attest to the fact that, for Latinos, especially, race and ethnicity are situational and contextual. Nevertheless, Latino immigrants, like all other immigrants, are affected by the racial hierarchy and racial ideology present in the United States. Even the process of becoming one ethnic group, "Latinos," is part of the racialization process, similar to the experience of Italian immigrants who never saw themselves as one ethnic group ("Italians") until they came to the United States. Individuals from many different backgrounds, who often only share a language, are recognizing the political and cultural benefits to being perceived as one large group. Therefore, this group, Latinos, is conceived in opposition to others, with the construction of "us" only possible by the construction of "them." For many immigrants, by continuing to recognize the desirability of whiteness, it means placing themselves higher on the racial and social hierarchy than black Americans.

Southern and Eastern European immigrants in the earlier part of the twentieth century went through a process of racialization intertwined with that of class status that resulted in a white racial identity. Immigrants today, largely composed of people from Asian and Latin American countries, also experience pressure to identify in racial terms; their racial identities are distinct from white, yet ambiguously nonwhite; they are neither white nor black but somewhere in between (Fernandez 2000, Kibria 1996, Lott 1998, Min and Kim 1999, Palumbo-Liu 1999, Piatt 1997). The ongoing interracial tensions we see in society today are, in part, due to this racial ambiguity, which arises out of people's different racial and class positions and their quest for preferred and privileged status in a racial hierarchy.

Conclusion

This chapter began with an overview of the racial social structure as it exists in the United States. This is the society into which new immigrants and their children are entering. Racial ideology rationalizes, justifies, and legitimates this racist and racial social structure. By exploring how this racial ideology was created and expressed to immigrants in the past, and its effect on their racial identities and racial knowledge, we can begin to understand the situation for the current wave of immigrants.

All immigrants, and their children, go through a process of assimilation into their new host society. While the assimilation process may be different for different groups of immigrants, what is consistent for all is that part of this process involves learning the current racial ideology. It is impossible to enter into a racist society and not become exposed to the racial ideology that supports this institutionalized racism. This learned racial ideology, which has a part in the assimilation process, then affects the racial identity process for new immigrants. Finally, through their own racial identity constructions as well as their understandings of how others are perceived racially in their new society, new immigrants help to reproduce the very system they have entered. This is what the rest of this book explores: first, how immigrants learn about this racial ideology and racial social structure while still in their home countries; how those they encounter in the host society contribute to the learning process; how immigrants then express this racial ideology; and, finally, how this ideology appears to affect their identities.

Note

1. I use the fictional name of "Eastern City" in order to further protect the identities of my participants.

3

Immigrants' Preconceptions of Race

In order to understand fully how immigrants learn the current racial ideology in the United States, we need to begin with an understanding of their previous knowledge about race in the United States. Therefore, this chapter takes a step back and briefly addresses the kinds of racial knowledge immigrants bring with them from their home countries. However, before exploring their preconceptions about race, racial categories, and the racial social structure in the United States, it is important to explain this all-encompassing concept of "immigrants."

Immigrants' Perceptions of Racism

As discussed in the first two chapters, immigrants entering the United States today are largely from Latin American and Asian countries. Obviously, however, the large number of immigrants entering and residing in the United States means they differ on a number of important levels. Significantly, immigrants vary in terms of their income, educational, and occupational levels. For example, although we may lump together Asian immigrants, there is a vast difference between an upper-income, professional Japanese immigrant coming for a top-level business position and a lower-income, far less educated Vietnamese immigrant. Clearly, these class differences will affect their assimilation patterns (as discussed briefly in the previous chapter), such as where they settle and the schools their children attend.

Additionally, immigrants vary a great deal—often in direct relation to their socioeconomic status—in terms of their knowledge and understanding of English. This, too, will affect their perceptions of the racial social structure in the United States. Several other factors will also likely affect their positions once they enter the country: their gender can have a pronounced influence on their assimilation and acculturation (Hondagneu-Sotelo 1994); their age and family structure (whether they immigrate alone or with family members); and, importantly, their status—whether they immigrate legally, as a undocumented resident, or as a refugee.

All of these factors can work together or independently to affect immigrants' interactions with native-born Americans, resulting in potentially very different understandings of the racial social structure in the United States. However, my goal is not to focus on how groups of immigrants (or individual immigrants) learn about race in the United States, but, instead, to explain some of the ways in which structural racism and racial ideology are passed on to new members of society, how immigrants interpret and make this knowledge their own, and how that process helps to reproduce the system into which they are entering. Therefore, while I clearly recognize that assimilation patterns will differ for different groups of immigrants (Portes and Rumbaut 2001), my intention here is to show how, regardless of the assimilation path taken, that path will always include an understanding and incorporation of the current racial ideology.

The next section explores how some of the immigrants I spoke with explained race and racism in their home countries. It is in this discussion that we can begin to see the way immigrants think about race here in the United States. No immigrant arrives free of any previous understanding of race; what is important is the way these previous conceptions work to aid in his or her construction of race in the United States.

Perceptions of Racism in the Home Countries

Although my argument is that immigrants acquire racial knowledge after immigrating to the United States, I also readily acknowledge that they arrive here with their own understandings about race and racism, often based on how racial identities and categories were defined in their home countries. For example, in Latin America, racial constructions are more fluid and based on things like class and phenotype (color, hair texture, facial features); Latinos bring these conceptions with them, which influence how they view their own and others' racial identities (Rodriguez 2000). And in Latin America, just like in the United States, these racial constructions have a relation to racism and power.

What became readily apparent was that most of those immigrants denying the existence of racism in this country made a point to contrast it with the racism they said existed in their countries of origin. For example, Lisa, from Colombia, mentioned several times during her interview that one of the things she liked so much about the United States was that "everyone is treated the same," in contrast to her view of racism toward blacks in Colombia.

> LISA: There is a lot of racism towards blacks. There is a lot of racism toward the black race. *[In Colombia?]* In Colombia. *[Not in the US?]* Here it seems everyone is treated the same. This is from what I see. . . . In my experience and in how long I have been here. I see that blacks, whites, or whatever they are, they are all treated the same. . . . [In Colombia,] there is a lot of racism toward the black race (and) the highest positions, the best jobs belong to white people. The black race does not appear to rise.

Her belief in the American Dream led her to perceive equal treatment with equal opportunity. However, people from the same country often made different claims about the existence of racism in their home countries. For example, Laura, who is also from Colombia, disagreed with Lisa's statements and said any problems in Colombia were strictly "military and ideological." As she explained, "In Colombia there exists different types of regions and each region has their own customs and their own way of living. . . . We all have the same insignia, that we are Colombians, and that we all struggle for the same thing." The different perceptions of racism in one's country are obviously not very different from the different perceptions native-born Americans hold about racism in the United States.

Some immigrants from Latin America said that there was little division in their countries based on race and that any existing distinctions often had more to do with class or politics. When it was about phenotype or color, they often said (as Laura did, above) that divisions had more to do with an individual's geographic location within the country. This was particularly the case for those immigrants from Peru, who said that most of the differences among groups depended on regional distinctions. All the Peruvians I spoke with repeated that there were three distinct regions in Peru: the coast, the mountains, and the jungle. They explained that people from each area looked down on the people from other areas. Occasionally they acknowledged that on some level racism did exist in their country, citing such examples as blacks not being allowed into certain private clubs. As Manny said, "I should also comment that in my country, black people distinguish themselves in every-thing—in the music, in sports—but are always discriminated against because of their color." Some of the Peruvian respondents were very clear and specific about the racism and in a similar way contrasted it with the lack of racism existing in the United States. For example, Karen said that she was specifically told by her Peruvian-American friend that one of the great things about the United States was that there was no racism, as there was in Peru.

Those who did discuss racism in their country often said race and class went "hand in hand." They claimed that whites held most of the positions of power in their countries and that often, even if a black person has money, he or she will still not be fully accepted. They would then consistently contrast the situation in their own countries with the situation in the United States, saying that whites did not hold all the power here and blacks of higher social classes were fully accepted in this country. Again, we see the strong relationship between the American Dream ideology and the belief that racism does not exist in the United States. For these immigrants, believing that the same situation exists here as in their countries, in terms of open social mobility or the lack thereof, would greatly negate their reasons for coming here. The strong belief in the American Dream is at odds with any belief in obstacles to that dream, such as racism.

Most of the immigrants I spoke with either claimed that racism did not exist in their home countries (and there were few distinctions in terms of a racial hierarchy), or, if it did, distinctions were more about politics or geography. For example, all of the West Indians I talked with said that racism did not exist in their countries and that divisions were based more on class or politics. As Lee, from Jamaica, explained:

> LEE: Yeah, [Jamaica's] a place where we never, we don't know about racial things, 'til I come here. No, we don't know them things there, until I come to America, that's where I know about people prejudice against people. 'Cause white company back home, blacks basically run them and you know, it's white company, everybody get along, we hang out in the club. Back home we with white girls like nothing. You see. Up here it's like, you go into some white area with a white girl, and like, Ehh, what's he doing? [*laughs*]

Nevertheless, later in his interview, Lee did acknowledge that he had occasionally encountered racism, or racists, in Jamaica, but he insisted that black Jamaicans just ignore it when they experience it.

At times, these immigrants' portrayals of their countries contradicted what some scholars have documented. For example, the two Cuban men I spoke with insisted that there was hardly any racism in Cuba, which is not quite the same argument scholars studying race and racism in Cuba make (de la Fuente 2001, Logan 1999). Additionally, Audrey, from Brazil, claimed there was very little racism in Brazil and that the racism that existed was directed at poor blacks and was alleviated by the organizations that existed to defend black people. Furthermore, she maintained that the racism in the United States was worse than that in Brazil. Similar to the discrepancy between the perceptions of the Cuban interviewees and those of scholars writing on race in Cuba, this report of minimal racism in Brazil is not necessarily consistent with what some scholars have described regarding race and racism in Brazil, where they argue that often racism is only more covert than it is in the United States (Marx 1998, Premdas 1995).

We also need to look carefully not just at what people say about race, but also at the context and words they use to discuss the various concepts (van Dijk 1993, 1987, 1985). Examining the discourse in this way provides insight into how individuals think about a certain situation, when their previous words may contradict these beliefs. For example, Stacy (Peru) described how, while she was not racist, she knew racism existed to some extent in Peru. She provided an example of the type of racism that might exist in terms of employment: "Even in the area of employment. Many times you could see that in the jobs. . . . Discrimination to a certain extent, it wasn't that obvious. Hiring a pretty, white receptionist versus a dark-skinned, fat receptionist." In the example she gave here, we must question why she contrasted the image of "pretty and white" with "dark-skinned and fat."

I saw another example of this type of contrast when an immigrant was describing her own parents. Ariel, from the Dominican Republic, said that racism did not exist in her country and that people did not "take into account" differences based on race or ethnicity. However, she then went on to answer questions about her parents in a most unusual way: "*{What are your parents in the DR?}* Dominicans. *{Dominicans. What race?}* In reality, my mother is white and very beautiful and my father is black and ugly. *{Why is he ugly?}* Because he's ugly. *{And your mother?}* Is beautiful."Again, we see terms relating to beauty and attractiveness being used in direct relation to issues about race. Ariel also claimed that while "there is no racism in the Dominican Republic," she remembered one particular club that did not allow people of color to enter. She said the name of this club was "Pretty."

Preconceptions of the United States
and Its Racial Hierarchy

There are a variety of possible ways for immigrants to begin learning about race and racial ideology in the United States. Obviously, exposure to US media is one such way immigrants may be exposed to US culture and ideologies before entering this country. Additionally, engaging in transnationalism, those who have already arrived here maintain ties to their home countries, thereby sharing information about what life is like here. If this is the case, we would expect information to be shared in both directions, and some of that information returning to the home country possibly would include mention of racial categories and racism in the new society. However, according to some scholars, such as Elliot Barkan (2006), this transnationalism is overstated and is, in fact, more like a Bell curve. "Most immigrants fall into the middle range, maintaining only limited, intermittent, episodic, financially uneven ties" (2006:15), which Barkan labels "translocalism." Further, as other scholars have noted (Mahler 1995), many immigrants do not want to admit anything negative about this new society they have worked hard to come to, preferring to paint their new home as desirable and worthy of the effort to immigrate. The next sections explore these varying contexts of previous knowledge: media and other institutional resources, and family and friends who immigrated earlier.

All of our major institutions have helped contribute to the ongoing racial ideologies. In particular, our media has consistently contributed to the dominant ideologies of racism in this country. Additionally, the media has had a greater impact on individuals around the world than have all other institutions.

Consistent with what we might think about the pervasiveness of US media outlets, about half of the immigrants I interviewed said they had watched a few US movies, watched news shows, and occasionally watched US television shows. For some, it was through the news in their own countries that they learned about issues in the United States. When asked whether she had ever heard that there was racism in the United States, Audrey, from Brazil, explained,

AUDREY: Yes. On TV. I'd seen it on TV. In Brazil. I knew that was a very big issue between black and white people in the United States, bigger than in Brazil. So it's black people in their area and white people in their area, so it's very separate.

However, the impact of the US media was not quite as pervasive as I expected, as some of the immigrants claimed they had never watched US movies or television and rarely read US newspapers before coming to the United States. This distinction definitely seemed to exist on more of a class level, with the more-middle-class immigrants seeming to have had more access to US media sources before migrating. According to all the immigrants, however, it appeared that the predominant informational resource for learning about the United States before their arrival was family and friends.

Some immigrants said they had heard and learned about the United States during their education. In the way some of the immigrants explained what they had learned, the information seems to have been very general.

> CRAIG (Colombian): When we were studying in the university we saw something about the history of the US. When you look at the history of America you see how this country developed. You see what groups came—they were basically the Europeans, the English, the Irish, the Scottish. Then there were the, well, the Indians were already here and then the blacks arrived.

In the way this immigrant explained it, the Europeans alone developed this country, and blacks just happened to arrive here, too. This is unfortunately similar to what I found in many of the tutoring resources I discuss in the next chapter; rather than discuss issues with these immigrants, such as the very important distinctions between those who came (and come) to this country out of choice versus those who were forced to come, the history of slavery is glossed over and minimized.

Most of these immigrants' education about the United States occurred at colleges where they took courses on world history or United States history. Some of the immigrants from Europe (specifically, France and Spain), Peru, Colombia, and Cuba mentioned professors talking about US history in their college and high school classes. As Lori, from France, explained, what she learned and what she saw were not always the same thing:

> LORI: I remember studying the civil rights movement, and the Black Panthers, and Martin Luther King, so I had assumed it was a very divided country where black people were poor and struggling. And here we come and the [black] gardener [in California] was driving

this huge, black car and seems to be quite well off. And that completely threw me. But then after that, that same summer, my cousin's wife took me to Watts and so then I had a very different impression. And that was more in keeping with what I'd imagined. But not that different than what I'd experienced in France with North Africans. . . . Although in France I don't think it's as divided as here.

Finally, some respondents talked about receiving information on the United States via government resources. Concerning the immigrants from Cuba, this source of knowledge was most often the case.

ANDY (Cuba): *{How did you know there was discrimination against blacks in the US?}* In class, we had a class in universal history. There the professor explains about the racial systems in Africa, then we jump to the US when the KKK existed. When Martin Luther King and all those things we learned in class regarding blacks.

One of the basic sources from which immigrants receive information about the United States are previous immigrants, such as family members and friends. Unfortunately, both sources tend to provide false or misleading, and often fantasy, information (Mahler 1995). Freddy gave a nice example of seeing this firsthand and it's worth repeating at length.

FREDDY (Peru): A lot of times when you have a poor person here when they write their homes, "Oh, I'm a dishwasher, I have a car, I have a TV, I have a house," and they believe that and I know by experience, because a lot of times when I used to go back to Lima, they used to tell me that, "Oh, as a dishwasher or cleaning tables in a restaurant you can make a lot of money." Say no, as a dishwasher or a cleaning lady you're gonna starve, you're gonna starve to death, you not gonna have a nice apartment. Oh no, but so and so and so and so and so and so, they doing that and they telling me they live like kings. And then they look at me like I'm lying. So after a couple years I was telling them the truth, I say forget it. They don't want to listen to the truth, they want to listen to what they want to hear. . . . Well, a lot of people come here with that idea that they gonna live like kings without working too hard. When they come here and they find out that it's not like that, well then, rather than say the truth, back home, well, it's not like that, you have to work your tail off to get something back. If you work hard you're gonna enjoy. But so when they come here thinking they gonna work very little and live like kings and when they find out the difference, that's part of the protest, not the country, not the way of living.

The majority of the people I interviewed claimed that any information they received about the United States primarily came from letters and phone calls with family and friends who had previously immigrated to the United States. Few of the immigrants I spoke with said they had had any previous contact with Americans before coming to the United States. Some said they had observed US tourists in their countries, others said they had had some degree of contact with Americans at US embassies, and only a few said they had had limited dealings with US soldiers (specifically, the Asian immigrant respondents). Some of the professional immigrants I spoke with had had experiences traveling in the United States before they immigrated, but, even then, the majority claimed not to have had much contact with native-born Americans. Instead, the majority explained that they had either remained with their families or travel groups at tourist locations, or they had sought out others from their same countries for friendship and assistance.

For the majority of immigrants, it was often one particular family member or friend who had provided the basis for information. For example, Laura, from Colombia, spoke at length about an aunt who had immigrated previously and who had subsequently helped convince her to come to the United States. As she explained, although she was scared to come here, "I knew that I was going to be with my aunt in one area that would not be a problem." Similarly, Theresa (Cambodia) spoke about a sister who had immigrated and had urged Theresa and her mother to do so also. Theresa described how, at first, she was confused about what she saw and heard about the United States, but then her sister came here and wrote to her about it in a positive way.

THERESA (Cambodia): I tell you that the people they know about like some TV, when we saw the picture, about the house, about the car, about the everything grow, you know, like the computer, light, phone, I am so confused. Like in my country we don't have that. My mother, she don't wanna come here, she said, "You can take your sister, your brother go there, oh I don't wanna go." Then my sister, she [come here] with her husband, explain about it, she took all the pictures, she had fun.

For some groups of immigrants, such as the Russian and Ukranian immigrants, their children who had immigrated before them were their primary source of information. They talked at length about their children's writing them letters and sending pictures of their homes and cars and how beautiful the United States always looked.

A major aspect of incorporating the current racial ideology is believing in the American Dream. The very reason most immigrants come to the United States is because of the power of this dream. They firmly believe that if they come here and work hard, boundless opportunities will exist and they will find a better economic future. This idea of meritocracy is firmly entrenched in modern racism, and was a concept discussed by many of the immigrants in my study.

Previous Knowledge of the American Dream

Interestingly, many of the immigrants I spoke with claimed to have had similar preconceptions of the United States as did the immigrants at the turn of the last century who wanted to immigrate to the "land paved with gold." In other chapters, we examine the power of the American Dream and the impact it has had on immigrants' perceptions of the potential for success and their explanations for people's failures. This chapter explores some of the first places the immigrants in my research began to learn about this dream.

With regard to learning about opportunities in the United States, family and friends, again, were clearly the primary sources of information. Regardless of whether the immigrants had watched US television shows popular in foreign countries, like *Baywatch* and *Dallas*, which portray inaccurate, sensationalized, and fantasy images of the United States, the most powerful source of immigrants' belief in becoming successful in the United States was from those who had immigrated previously. As Lisa, from Colombia, said, "[My friends] would say it was really good here, it was easy to get money. In a short period of time you could have the power to attain things—things that you've always wanted—easily." Another immigrant described what her relatives told her:

ARIEL (Dominican): They always painted it as the best place in the world. There were many opportunities and they say there was a lot of work. Here you would work and return back home in a year and enjoy your money and buy a house. These were the plans of every normal person. They would say [the United States] was fabulous and when was I planning to apply for a visa to come here. That you can succeed here and that was the only way for me to get ahead, to have a family and live differently.

And in words we might have heard from Irish or Italian immigrants in the early 1900s, Claire, from Jamaica, said, "Men used to come here and they used to come back and they make it seem like you can just come here and pick money off the tree." Often, it was the success of those who had previously immigrated that predicted the belief in the dream. For many of the Russian and Ukrainian immigrants, as well as several older Asian immigrants I talked with, their children and grandchildren had succeeded in obtaining good jobs, relatively (to their previous lifestyle) large homes, and often college educations.

Other times it was the lack of success of those left behind that inspired someone to leave and come to the United States. For example, Freddy, from Peru, previously a jockey, explained:

> FREDDY: Your future over there is very limited as a rider. You only have one, maybe two, major tracks, and if you don't do well in those two tracks then you are going to struggle . . . while here in the States, the purses were very good all over the country. . . . Opportunities much, much better. . . . I am, I make that move, 'cause when I go back to Lima and go to the racetrack I see exriders that did extremely well and I can tell they have a rough life, so here your opportunities—after you stop riding, you have so many opportunities, not perhaps to make the same kind of living when you were riding horses but you are not going to be in the poorhouse. While over there, most of them, they're struggling. Financially, not that well.

Aside from the more general questions I asked about previous knowledge and awareness of the United States, I also asked about diversity, discrimination, or race problems in the United States. Some immigrants said they had had no prior idea about the different racial and ethnic groups here, as explained by Audrey.

> AUDREY (Brazil): *{Would your aunt tell you anything about how diverse it was here?}* No, I didn't know, I was surprised. She did tell me that here they have a lot of Hispanic people. But I didn't know it was anything like that.

Other immigrants talked about being told of the extent of diversity and said they appreciated the variety of people from all over the world. For almost all of those I spoke with, this diversity was very different from what they had experienced in their home countries.

> KAREN I (Peruvian): Before I arrived I was very aware that this country is very diverse ethnically in regards to culture as well as the fact that this country has a lot to offer. It gives people the opportunity to come here and get a job, therefore you find people from all nationalities, all races, all religious beliefs. This country is very diverse. . . . [My boyfriend told me] that it was very diverse. The country is host to people from diverse racial backgrounds from all over the world. In the US, specifically in New York, you can find a diverse number of cultures—Chinese, Japanese, Peruvian, Colombians, Uruguayans, Europeans, Spanish, everything. You find everything.

What is important about this awareness of racial and ethnic diversity is its connection to the American Dream ideology. Hearing about and seeing all the different people in the United States reinforced for these immigrants the idea that anyone can make it here, regardless of his or her background. As Karen went on to say, "[My boyfriend would] say that he saw that in the US any person of color, Indians, Cholo or black, if professional, could accomplish any goal. This was something he did not see in Peru." Jesse also discussed hearing about the diversity in the United States when he was still in Mexico.

> JESSE: From all the countries—at every corner you would find someone from one country and at another corner you'd find someone from another country. You could find people from all the races in this country. They referred to it as the capital of the world. That's what they called it, the capital of the world. There was everything in the US.

For Jesse, his friends and family were making a connection between diversity and the potential for success.

Some of the interviewed immigrants said they heard about problems with discrimination in general, and with racism more specifically. However, some of those who heard about problems with racism claimed that it was not true. Some of Lisa's friends and family—who had been to the United States previously, or who had friends and family here already—told her not to come because of the discrimination here. However, Lisa (Colombian) said they told her the discrimination was toward Colombians specifically, not toward blacks; then she went on to say that she herself had never experienced any discrimination.

Occasionally problems with racism in the United States were heard about, not from friends or family, but from political figures. Both of the Cuban men I interviewed talked about how the Cuban government promoted the idea that racism existed in the United States. Aaron, however, believed the government's discourse about racism toward blacks in the United States was used to scare people from coming here and to bias them against the US political system.

> AARON: In my country, they talk a lot and say there is a lot of racism in the US. Cuba, and this is well known throughout the world, attacks the US regarding the racial problems. They say blacks are discriminated against here in the US, and that is not true. Politics in Cuba are based on saying that there is racism in the US. But of course, one who has never left Cuba cannot see that, they can't grasp it. A lot of people know it is not so because they receive visits from the US in Cuba or they get mail and they learn that it is not so.

Aaron claimed that the Cuban government's views are propaganda and Andy, also from Cuba, seemed to concur:

> ANDY: I knew it existed because I learned about it in school and I always paid attention to those things. I knew they exaggerated a little bit when they'd say there was discrimination in the US; they'd say that you couldn't go out to the streets late at night, they'd throw the dogs at you, they'd do things to you. I knew there was discrimination but only to a certain extent and I was able to understand. I'd say, I know there is discrimination but not as much, not in this day and age. Not at that level.

Andy said he learned this from government-sponsored school programs, and, like Aaron, he believed this racism does not exist to the extent he was told.

Occasionally an immigrant would talk specifically about being warned of the relationship between her or his own group and black Americans. Jesse, from Mexico, said he was warned by other Mexicans that "the blacks always had problems with us. *{With Mexicans?}* Yes, they would say that [blacks] would rob us and there were problems. They would warn me and say that it was good, but there also a lot of bad. *{Would they only mention the problems with the blacks? Did they*

ever mention anything about whites?} No, they never mentioned anything about whites." Manny, from Peru, also said he was told black people believed they were discriminated against by anyone who looked at
them and so he should be wary of interactions with them.

Conclusion

The immigrants I interviewed received knowledge about life in the
United States from family and friends who had come before them; and
although they often discovered falsehoods in these letters and phone
calls, these sources of information were what they had to rely on before
their arrival. Once they did arrive, as seen in the next chapter, they discovered a world full of segregation—in neighborhoods, schools,
employment, and friendships. We can begin to see how previous racial
knowledge, in combination with discovery of a new racial hierarchy
(learned, in part, from agents of organizations they encounter), affect
new immigrants' various racialization processes. The next chapter
examines how the current racial ideology, modern racism, is expressed
by native-born Americans to new immigrants. An important part of the
assimilation process for immigrants, native-born Americans play a
major role in how immigrants come to understand race and race relations in the United States.

4

Seeing, Hearing, and Acquiring New Notions of Race

IMMIGRANTS LEARN ABOUT RACE IN THE United States in a variety of ways. As discussed in the previous chapter, they obviously do not enter their new host society completely unaware of its race relations environment and racial hierarchy. Additionally, they bring with them their own conceptions of race as created in their home countries. Once they arrive here, they begin to learn more about US racial social structure, racism, and racial hierarchy. They learn from those who immigrated here before them, they witness the experiences of those around them, they talk to other immigrants as well as native-born citizens, and they observe with their own eyes how we all live.

Making sense of this racial-information acquisition includes examining the specific cultural resources used by those helping immigrants in their acclimation process. For example, most major cities, and even small towns, now provide English as a Second Language (ESL) classes. Sometimes these are offered at the local library, along with other practical tips and hints to further the Americanization process. At other times, these are offered at centers specializing in immigrant services. Thus, one way we can understand how immigrants learn this racial ideology is by talking to the native-born workers providing these services.

It quickly became apparent from my interviews that, for many of the immigrants, these agents were the only native-born Americans they encountered on a regular, comfort-level basis. Therefore, the racial segregation they were witnessing and the racial ideology they were learning came largely from the immigrant-services organizations and the agents of these organizations that they were encountering. Immigrants learn the racial ideology not only from what people (native- and nonnative-born) say, but from what the immigrants see. A severe racial segregation exists at many of these immigrant services, which provides immigrants with a further understanding about US race relations and the US racial hierarchy. For example, if the majority of native-born Americans they encounter are white, and these are the people in administrative and tutorial positions, then immigrants learn who is in a superior status position.

As discussed in prior chapters, and as numerous scholars have attested, the majority of native-born white Americans express a modern racism ideology. Encompassed in this ideology are the beliefs that everyone is treated equally (color-blind racism), that no legislation or policies should ensure this equal treatment, that any socioeconomic discrepancies between racial groups are due to the cultural or natural deficiencies of the groups in the lower socioeconomic positions, and anyone who works hard can and will succeed. The majority of those I spoke with who work and volunteer at the immigrant-services agencies are native-born white Americans; it stands to reason we would see this ideology being expressed to the immigrants. As we saw in the previous chapter, the majority of the immigrants' friends and family members also attested to this ideology—in particular, the American Dream component (anyone who works hard can succeed). So, immigrants' racial ideology awareness and incorporation are affected by the native-born Americans they encounter as well as by previous immigrants. Both of these sources are expressing modern racism.

Immigrant Services and Organizations

The majority of my research for this work was conducted at a literacy center in the Northeast. While this center used to primarily serve illiterate adults in the area, in recent years it has correctly recognized the increased need for English as a Second Language classes and now offers more of these than English literacy classes. I did my research at the main center as well as at four of the satellite centers. Over a two-year period, I conducted personal interviews with immigrants and those working with immigrants; led one focus group with Asian immigrants; observed participants in numerous ESL classes; attended every party or function held at the main center; had informal conversations; and generally "hung around." Additionally, I analyzed immigrant students' writings (from the center), information from websites of local immigrant-services organizations, and the resources used by the tutors and administrators of the literacy centers.

By examining not only what immigrants have to say about their experiences, but also the institutions and organizations they come into contact with, we can better sort out how the racial reproduction process occurs. Institutions and organizations shape immigrant racial awareness and racial knowledge in much the same way they shape these understandings of the native-born members of society. Investigating the immigrant experience allows us to examine the racial reproduction process nearer to the time it first begins to develop. By highlighting the process as it occurs for immigrants, it is possible that we will then be better able to understand this process for all members of society.

Numerous services within most major cities provide services to and for immigrants. Immigration and naturalization services (formerly INS; now known as CIS, Citizenship and Immigration Services) exist in practically every city to address citizenship requirements and to provide documents pertaining to work and residency status. Additionally, there are various other social-service agencies, nonprofit organizations, and religious services designed to assist immigrants within the local community. I discuss two such services: one is a program conducted under the auspices of the main city library (but funded by a private, nonprofit organization) and one is a nonprofit organization providing language and citizenship classes to immigrants. The latter, Literacy Volunteers of Eastern City (LVEC), is where I conducted the majority of my observations.[1]

These two services provide examples of how immigrants receive racial knowledge. What we see, particularly from the library service, is that intricately related to racial knowledge is knowledge about "Americanness." Threaded throughout the mission statements and texts used by both services is the notion of who, and what, is an American, as well as the concept of the American Dream. Both services strongly support the notion that those who work hard can overcome any struggle, and that to do so is to be truly American. This belief is a central component of the modern racism ideology.

Eastern City Library

The services the main public library in Eastern City provides emphasize the ideas of Americanness and assimilation. Called "The American Place," the service is described as an "International Welcome Center." The resources provided include citizenship preparation, ESL classes, and "life skills" workshops. In essence, the founders of this service see themselves as assisting the immigrant in making as smooth an assimilation as possible. As the opening quote from historian Eric F. Goldman, listed on their website and in published statements, says, "The American public library empowered many immigrants to transform their individual dreams and potentialities into American realities."

There is no doubt that this community service provides much-needed practical resources—such as citizenship classes, passport services, and information on immigration laws and refugee rights—for newcomers to Eastern City. However, we can also determine from the title and from the cultural resources the program provides that there is another, more latent agenda and consequences of this service. Essentially, this program teaches newcomers, in addition to what is physically entailed in becoming an American, what it *means to be* an American and what it means to achieve the American Dream. As one staff member explained the need for the program, "We can't have the same kind of library that existed when you and I grew up." Here she is implying (and assuming that I am a white, native-born American, since we were speaking on the phone) that it is now the library's job to impart "American wisdom" to new immigrants. As it says in the library's mission statement, "The assimilation process must provide transition into mainstream American society for both immigrants-by-choice and immigrants-by-need."

This service certainly must be lauded for its attempts to aid the often difficult process of immigration and citizenship as well as for its desire to "preserve elements of native culture." However, the immigration services the library provides continue to promote and reinforce the ideas of open social mobility in the United States. The website provides several links to other sites regarding immigration and encourages immigrants to seek out information on these sites. For example, there is a link to "All-American Food and Recipes," as well as one simply called "Living in the United States." The American Place website recently included a lengthy discussion of social mobility in the United States:

> Unlike most countries, though, except at the very highest level, it is possible for an American to move up to a higher social class one step, or one generation at a time. Immigrants from many countries have arrived by the millions, started at the bottom of the ladder, and within a generation or two have become part of the mainstream of American middle class life.

What these types of statements do, essentially, is tell newcomers that anyone who works hard enough can make it, thereby reinforcing the idea that if there are people who are not making it, then it is their own fault—in other words, blaming the victim.

Another aspect to the library's website is a significant amount of information for ESL instructors. The site provides links to classes (such as at LVEC), stories and writings by immigrants, and suggested questions and conversation topics for instructors. The excerpts are predominantly about hard work and success; for example, it contains lengthy quotes from those who recount stories of struggles and hardships overcome. While the suggested topics for the ESL instructors could be helpful as well as be areas in which to encourage native-born English speakers to discuss potential difficulties with the newcomers, there is limited mention of racism or discrimination. The approximately forty subject areas include one titled "Social Problems"; here I found the only mention of race, racism, or discrimination. Furthermore, these terms make up only five questions out of over three dozen under "Social Problems." This downgrading of topics that could potentially be very important for recent immigrants reinforces the idea that race is not something that should be or will be important for immigrants and is not a topic on which ESL teachers should spend much time. What is of utmost importance here is to recognize that what is not said, or expressed, is every bit as important as what is. By not including racial identity or racism as significant topics of discussion with immigrants, native-born Americans are reinforcing color-blind ideology.

Much of what I observed at LVEC followed the same basic format as that of the library: focus on the effects of hard work and success, provide limited discussion about race or racism, and minimize the lack of real social mobility in the United States.

Literacy Volunteers of Eastern City

Organizational structure. Literacy Volunteers of Eastern City (LVEC) is a private, nonprofit, local center that provides a variety of resources for individuals in the community. While it was founded in 1972 mainly to provide literacy services to adults in the greater Eastern City area, the staff members quickly began to see the need to provide English classes to immigrants. Currently, two-thirds of its clientele, mostly foreign-born, are non–English speakers. Over two hundred immigrants use the services provided by LVEC. According to statistics collected by LVEC, in 1999, the student body was 48 percent Hispanic (Puerto Rican and Latin American), 32 percent black (African-American, West Indian, and African), 12 percent Caucasian (European immigrants and European-American), and 8 percent Asian.

While its primary service is giving literacy lessons, the center sees itself as providing for other needs as well. Its mission statement reads:

"[LVEC] creates opportunities for [Eastern City–] area adults to learn to read, write and speak English; to gain new ways to represent themselves; and to expand their contribution to their families and communities." Similar to the library resource center, LVEC provides various English-level classes, citizenship classes, computer-assisted English-language resources, and "an opportunity for individuals from various communities to interact with one another." As Greg, a native-born white administrator, said: "We are as important as a resource for cultural assimilation as we are for language development, if not more so. *{What do you mean by 'cultural assimilation'?}* Well, learning what they need to learn and feel they need to learn in order to live successfully in the new setting—language and cultural setting."

There is one main center and four established satellite centers (these only provide ESL and literacy classes). The main center houses the administrative staff, bulletin boards with announcements about upcoming events and important resources, citizenship classes, computer classes, and special events and programs. The majority of students use this center.

LVEC is an example of an organization structured in much the same way that most organizations in a racialized society are structured. A division exists between the students and staff, at both the main center and the satellite centers, that, when we look more closely, we see is along racial and ethnic lines. In particular, both the main center and the satellite centers have white-dominated administrative staff and tutors.[2] Importantly, as will be explained below, when students first contact the center, they are not told where they will take classes; instead, they are asked to choose the location of their courses.

One center (Center A), located in a predominantly black-American section of Eastern City, focused largely on literacy classes. Although there was a small Spanish-speaking population in this area of the city, there were only black Americans and West Indian immigrant students attending classes there. Out of six tutors, one was a native-born black American (a former student); another native-born black American tutor had just begun to volunteer when I left the center after more than six months of observation. A second center (Center B), also located in an area largely comprising native-born black Americans as well as West Indians, was located in a Salvation Army center and primarily served Russian and Ukrainian immigrants. About forty-five adults used this center, where English classes were offered once a week. Three of the tutors were native-born white Americans and one was a white English immigrant. A third center (Center C), located in a largely Spanish-speaking community, provided services to Asian immigrants from a variety of backgrounds, such as Chinese, Vietnamese, and Cambodian. At this center there was one native-born black American tutor and the rest were either Asian (native-born or English-speaking immigrants) or native-born white Americans.

The final center where I conducted observational research was the main center, where the majority of the immigrant students attended classes (Center D). At this center, most of the students were from Latin America, with some from various Asian countries. Out of approximately fifteen to twenty tutors, there was one Latino substitute tutor, one Latino who taught the citizenship classes, and two black tutors—one West Indian and one native-born black American—both of whom taught the literacy classes. The rest of the tutors were native-born white Americans. We can get a further idea of the racial structure of this organization by looking at the main center's administrative staff. Out of eight to nine full- and part-time staff members, there were two Latinas and one native-born black American woman. One Latina worked as the administrative secretary and the other worked in the evenings as the secretary and coordinator of evening classes. The native-born black American woman worked in various capacities: substitute tutor, computer laboratory coordinator, and general assistant to the reading center manager.

We might understand why the centers mirrored the racial segregation in Eastern City if students were taking classes near to where they resided. However, I witnessed students go out of their way to attend a particular center when a different one would have been more convenient. For example, I drove a West Indian immigrant home from her classes at Center A after she had missed her usual ride home with her tutor. After driving more than ten minutes to her home, I realized we were within walking distance of Center B. When I asked her why she went out of her way to attend Center A (and pointing out Center B to her), she first said she did not know, but later said she went there because her friends did. Similarly, at Center B, I witnessed the majority of immigrants either carpooling to the center or taking the bus, when the main center was much closer to most of their homes. And although many of the Russian and Ukrainian immigrants at Center B were older and possibly used the senior services also offered at this site, I encountered many older immigrants at the other sites as well. These other older immigrants, many Latino and West Indian, would certainly have benefited from the services offered at Center B, yet they had seemingly relinquished it to the Eastern European immigrants.

Self-segregation mirrors the larger society's racial segregation in many ways. As Douglas Massey and Nancy Denton established, "When it comes to housing and residential patterns . . . race is the dominant organizing principle" (1993:114). There is little reason to believe that when it comes to social interactions, race would not also be a dominant organizing factor. Camille Zubrinsky and Lawrence Bobo highlight, through their own analysis of residential segregation, that all groups claim to want both integration and a significant number of same-group neighbors (1996). Race matters not only because groups prefer "their own kind," "but because everyone is aware of and must adapt to the historically developed, structurally rooted, and psychologically unavoidable American racial order or hierarchy" (1996:372). This awareness and adaptation to the racial order appears to occur even in the seemingly insignificant decisions of newcomers choosing where to take English classes.

Additionally, I witnessed this self-segregation *within* classes. For example, in one class that had seven students, the students from similar backgrounds sat together and talked mostly to each other when the teacher was not talking. Interestingly, although they did not speak the same language, a student from Vietnam and a student from China worked together and helped each other with problems.

Various inferences can be made from this self-segregation among the students and the racial demographics of the tutors and staff. In terms of the former, students had limited contact with those who are different from themselves or their pan-ethnic/racial groups. Those who at one time might have had nothing in common with people of certain nationalities, or even might have been antagonistic toward a particular group—as one of the tutors believed was the case with the Russian and Ukrainian immigrants—were now bonded by their apparent similarities, basically indicating, "We are closer to each other than we are to any other group." This self-segregation, then, consolidated racial consciousness. For these Eastern European immigrants, their status as white immigrants now bonded them in a much stronger way than their differences over various nationalities separated them. Furthermore, except for Center A, which had a strong black American presence among the mostly West Indian and African student population, most immigrants had limited contact with native-born black Americans, a primary racial minority group in the United States and Eastern City. Even at this center, however, the West Indian immigrants had a biased perception of native-born black Americans as a group low in socioeconomic status, because of the latters' position in this center as "illiterate" students.

For the immigrants using the centers, the racial composition among the staff and tutors represented US society's racial hierarchy and racial stratification. Additionally, for most of the students, the tutors were not only predominantly white, but were native-born Americans. Often, these tutors were the few US citizens with whom the immigrants ever came into direct, speaking contact, because of the immigrants' lack of English-language proficiency. As several of the immigrant respondents pointed out, they did not speak to Americans outside of the center because of their fear of being misunderstood.

The process of acquiring racial knowledge does not necessarily include being openly told of a racist practice, but may involve witnessing the practice firsthand. Using the center's resources, immigrants observe an organization structured along racial lines. The predominance of a white-dominated administrative staff further reinforces the idea that Americanness equates whiteness, and, hence, whiteness indicates a position of privilege and power. By examining this organization, we can see this relationship between whiteness and Americanness as well as a clear example of one more white-dominated organization in a white-dominated society.

Cultural Resources

In texts, just like in speech, what is missing is often as important as what is said. When a tutor tells his students that they need not concern themselves with discussions about race, this message is as important as what *is* discussed. Part of the current racial ideology, passed on through culture and cultural agents, is the notion of color-blindness: the idea that individuals in the United States do not see skin color, that everyone is treated equally regardless of their color, and that discrimination based on color/race does not exist. In our white-dominated society, racism is constantly dismissed as nonexistent. Within the organization I studied, this message was repeated. By ignoring questions or concerns about race or racism in a very similar manner to the library's resources, the largely white staff and tutors appeared to support this denial of racism.

Tutor training manuals.   Before the tutors began to teach their own classes, they went through a two-week orientation and training process. They trained twice each week for three-and-a-half hours at a time (including in-class observation). One upper-level staff member (Greg, native-born white American) and his assistant (Yolanda, native-born black American) taught the training classes. The manual that accompanied the training provided insights into what the staff believed were key pieces of knowledge for future tutors to know and to provide to their students.

The locally constructed manual, largely created by Greg, has several sections. It begins with four case studies of typical students coming to use the services of LVEC.[3] Each of the four stories highlights the struggles that individuals encounter in their lives and the hard work and determination it takes to learn English. The next section discusses the mission and purposes of LVEC and includes a paragraph about how volunteers are not only teaching people English, but also enabling people from different cultures and backgrounds to come together and meet, people who would ordinarily not have the opportunity to do so. Essentially, this introduction reinforces the idea that US ideologies—hard work and determination, combined with a cultural pluralism—are uniquely US attributes, and encourages the tutor to incorporate these ideas into the classroom.

In a discussion more specifically about ESL learners, as opposed to literacy learners, the manual includes a paragraph underscoring the recognition that learning English also means learning about cultural norms and US institutions, as well as about how US systems work, to encourage immigrants to participate actively in these systems. Here we see a clear acknowledgment on the part of the staff that they are cultural agents, imparting cultural knowledge to immigrants through their interactions. Furthermore, the manual encourages the future tutors to engage students (immigrants) in learning the language for a variety of contexts they are likely to encounter in the "target culture." Additionally, a final paragraph regarding teaching in context notes that cultural understanding must also be promoted so that the students are sensitive to other cultures and thus may live more harmoniously in the new environment.

The idea of learning in contexts could provide the opportunity to discuss experiences of race, racial identity, racism, discrimination, or prejudice. However, there are few examples of such discussions. Some exceptions can be found to this lack of information about race (in any capacity: race, racism, racial identity) in the manual; specifically, there is a brief discussion about social identity and the changes individuals may go through after they come to live in the United States. Within this context, tutors are encouraged to talk to their students about the changes they experience and how their new identities are influenced by a variety of factors, some of which they have control over and some they do not—but that, overall, they have some choice in who they become.

These ideas of social identity include concepts of national identity, gender identity, sexual orientation, and racial identity. Another mention of racism was collapsed into a discussion of ethnocentrism, alongside mention of sexism and prejudice in general. I want to reiterate my previous comment: *Language is important for what is not said just as much as for what is said.* By not including conversations about the racism immigrants may or may not encounter, the staff was essentially promoting color-blind racism (a component of modern racism), asserting that we live in a society where no one sees or recognizes race. Members of racial majority groups are in the privileged position of not having to "see" race or acknowledge the existence of racism. For the native-born, white staff member who created the tutor training manual, race and racism are largely unimportant and irrelevant concepts for future members of US society.

Some exceptions exist to the lack of attention on race and racism in the tutor training materials. For example, one of the manuals, which focuses largely on potential lesson plans, includes a discussion of similarities and dissimilarities between West Indians and African-Americans. However, this aspect of the manual is centered on literacy volunteers who would be teaching either native-born Americans or English speakers how to read and write English. While a discussion of similarities or differences between West Indians and black Americans points in a positive direction since it provides a contextual base for conversations about race among West Indians, it still does not provide for this conversation among tutors teaching English to non-English-speaking immigrants. Additionally, mentioning potential parallels between only these two groups and not any other groups promotes a stereotypical idea that only black immigrants and native-born black Americans have any commonalities. Again, this is consistent with the sensibilities of the larger white majority, where, when race is seen, it is primarily a "black issue."

A major part of tutor training involved enforcing the idea that the immigrant students should learn from one another and that their learning experience was grounded in their actual experiences. Included in the training manual, then, are suggested topics for conversation. With major categories suggested, including culture, children, education, immigration, family, neighborhoods, health, employment, and politics, the only mention of racism is under the categories of "Neighborhoods" and "Quality of Life." In addition to these suggested conversation topics and promoting the idea of immigrants' learning from one another, the tutors were instructed to rely heavily on the writings of previous and current immigrant students.

The overwhelming majority of student writings focus on how grateful and happy the immigrants were to be learning English and to be in the United States, where they could make a better life for themselves. Stories tell of the immigrants' struggles in their home countries, especially among Asian immigrants, many of whom came as refugees. Students from Central and South America and the West Indies tell of poverty and a desire to make a better life for themselves. The writings focus on their determination to learn English, on the improvements in their lives when they did finally learn English, and on the potential for anyone to succeed in the United States. As one Jamaican woman wrote, "If we could overcome these obstacles, so can everyone else who wants to do good for themselves." Essentially, the immigrants themselves and the use of their stories in the classroom reinforced the US ideologies of hard work and determination. Furthermore, these stories support, in a latent fashion, the idea that those who are not succeeding are failing through some fault of their own—another major tenet of modern racism.

Agents of the Organization

Staff responses to racial segregation.   Some of the staff members recognized the issues of racial segregation and division. While most talked about his or her own role as either a white person or a person of color working with immigrants, some staff members commented on the segregation among the students.

> BONNIE (native-born white American): I think connections are natural. I studied in Spain and we—Americans—used to congregate together. It's natural. But I think everyone gets along, they can be interested to learn about someone new, like learning about Vietnam. But you wouldn't see a Vietnamese inviting a Latino over for dinner [*laughs*].

Here, Bonnie, an upper-level administrator at LVEC, recognized the segregation, but did not see it as problematic. However, Greg, another upper-level administrative staffer who was a native-born white American, talked at some length about the benefits the students received by having the opportunity to learn about one another's cultures and share experiences with each other.

> GREG: Being able to connect with other people—both within their own cultural language group and others—in order to meet more of

their own needs and aspirations and sense of who they are . . . I
think that sense of, and that connectivity, can manifest itself in some
very sharp survival or it can be something much more diffuse and
aesthetic, and anywhere in between. . . . And the classes are more
the multicultural meeting place where—they're more multicultural
in orientation and so people, there's a common sense of "We need
English," if you will, or, you know, "We are learning to adjust and
to assimilate." . . . But what I pick up is, for the most part, I don't
see a lot of barriers between different groups working with each
other here [the main center] or in the community program. And, for
the most part, people are curious or it's the class group itself which
becomes the focal point for work and engagement and that kind of
thing. And it's less that "This person is Hispanic," "This person is
Asian," "This person is from Haiti"—whatever. That seems not to
be a big deal, frankly.

Nonetheless, after having expressed this potential for shared experiences, Greg went on to talk about how the opportunity to learn from one
another did not occur very often, and used the Russians at Center B and
the Southeast Asians going to Center C as examples of this self-segregation. It seems here that while some of the staff members thought LVEC
offered the potential for learning about and understanding other cultures, they recognized that self-segregation did exist and yet did not
seem to feel any need to adjust this segregation. Furthermore, Greg,
even after he was pushed to explain the segregation, insisted it had more
to do with factors other than race or ethnicity.

GREG: I think differences have more to do with age, one's own
background, educational background, vocational background—
background, just level of sophistication and awareness. How much
money a person has, resources a person has or doesn't have, I mean,
I think those are the more fundamental issues.

While I agree that there might be numerous factors that affect self-
segregation, what I witnessed at the various centers attested to the fact
that race and ethnicity played a major role in this self-segregation. For
example, looking at the Russian and Ukrainian immigrants at Center B,
some of them told stories of being doctors, engineers, and high-level
scientists in their home countries, while others told stories of poverty
and low-level jobs. Yet here in the United States, their similar ethnicities
overrode all class and occupational status differences.

It is difficult not to see similarities between this segregation among adult learning centers and our country's ongoing school segregation. In much the same way, both sets of students are learning from and with others who look similar to them, are from similar backgrounds and cultures, and will not challenge their accepted beliefs and ideologies in any significant manner. As numerous school segregation studies have argued, "Desegregated schools help teach Latino, African American, Asian, and white youngsters to function together in the workplace and to coexist in harmony in an increasingly diverse society" (Piliawsky 1998). There's no reason to believe that desegregated ESL classes for adults would not have the same positive effects.

More often than not, the discussion about lack of diversity came from the few racial minorities among the staff and centered on the staff and tutors as examples of racial divisions. As Maggie, one of the Latina staff members said to me, "It would be good to have Latino and African-Americans working here because then [the students] are seeing others who look like them." For Maggie, as a Latina, there was a clear need for more tutors who resembled the students they were teaching. She believed the students saw her as one of them and that this affected their relationships in that it made the students more open and expressive with her. Although she was talking primarily about the students from Latin America, she also said she believed there needed to be more native-born black American tutors as well. Yolanda, the native-born black American staff member, also talked about the need for more "brown faces," as she put it. She did, however, claim that there were more native-born black American tutors now than when she began five or six years ago. When she said that was a good thing, I asked her why.

YOLANDA: Well, I just think sometimes—sometimes it's important for people to see people who are like themselves, not just, I mean, basic literacy students. Most of the students are either from one of the islands, Jamaica or something, the West Indies, or might be, you know, African-American. But I think also, and even for Latinos . . . some people are a little bit browner in complexion. Some are fair in complexion. So, but I think even for them, as well, sometimes to see someone they might resemble—even having Maggie here, because she speaks Spanish and is also a Latino—because sometimes there are things culturally that you don't know how to explain to other people. . . . But I've had students who are from the [predominantly African-American] area say things to me, feeling that I might understand better because I'm also a person of color, whereas to try to explain to their tutor who's from [a predominantly European-American town] and is white—they just want me to listen and have a perspective of understanding, but not the same thing as maybe just a person who culturally grew up. And it really—I mean, I don't know how much it has to do with color because, on the one hand, yes, I'm African- American. So there's a certain cultural identity that I have.

She further explained that this shared cultural identity might not necessarily exist even if there were shared racial identity.

YOLANDA: But I also grew up in a suburban area and there's a totally different culture there that I would know nothing about had I been African-American growing up in the [predominantly African-American] area of [Eastern City]. But what bonds myself and a literacy student from [the predominantly African-American area] of [Eastern City] is the fact that we're both African-American. And in some ways we might have shared some African-American cultural experience that, you know, be it the foods, the language, family, how people get along—whatever—so that we understand and it's— you can find a way to relate.

Here we see Yolanda struggling with the idea that a shared racial identity might supersede cultural differences. She clearly recognized the need for students to see "others who look like them," yet simultaneously recognized that that might not be enough.

Some of the white tutors, however, did not necessarily see the issue the same way. For example, Patty, a tutor for numerous years at Center A, the predominantly black American and West Indian center, and an immigrant herself (from England), believed the predominance of white tutors was partly positive and partly problematic because of how it provided integration to the center.

PATTY: That's why I think these family resource centers are the way to go, if only they could make them more integrated, 'cause, you know, I got to know everybody here and we're all friends now and that's how it works, it's not something that can happen overnight. . . . It's a double-edged sword because you want them to have more teachers of their predominant background . . . but also you want some sort of integration, so it's very difficult. I don't know what the answer to that is.

While Patty seemed to recognize her whiteness status, in terms of saying that she provided integration into the environment, she also claimed not to see her whiteness.

> PATTY: I don't think actually a lot of color, I mean, I don't think I'm white. I don't know, I suppose when I first came [to the center] it was more of a feeling that I was usually the only white person here, but it never worried me because I'd worked in that sort of setting a lot before and now I don't even think about it.

It is certainly interesting that Patty used the word "worried" to describe her feelings, or lack of feelings, about being at the center. Another white tutor appeared much more aware of her whiteness status and the role that status played among the students she tutored. Polly, a native-born American, said she recognized that her students saw her as a white person and that it was possible many of her students had had negative experiences with "people who looked like me." However, Polly clarified her statement by saying she had noticed the recognition of her white status mostly among her students from the Caribbean, where they expressed the message that white people thought they were better than black people and that black people did the jobs whites would not do. Polly, like Patty, said the diversity the students received with each other in the classroom was a good thing; as she put it, "They get to be with a real cross-section of people, including the instructor." Similar to Maggie's comments, though, Polly also believed there was a need for more diversity among the staff, particularly among the higher-level administrative staff.

> POLLY: I personally would like to see some diversity at the head office. There are two wonderful women who are there . . . in the night program that I observe were treated like handmaidens, not held in very high regard—just two women who are willing to work, you know, night hours. I'd like to see some women of color running the program, having something to do with the program.

When I asked her, Polly explained that the two women in question were both women of color and were being treated poorly—not by students, but by the upper-level staff members. Polly also claimed to have heard racist comments from some of those running the program and said she occasionally heard these comments made in front of the students.

I spoke with one woman from whom Polly claimed to have heard racist comments. Neither this woman nor the other upper-level administrator I spoke to appeared to recognize their whiteness in their interactions with students. In both interviews, although commenting on their family ancestry, neither mentioned the fact that they were white and how this might affect the students. Even more, they both commented on their own ancestry, one Polish and one Greek, and how that European ancestry had fallen away to where they simply saw themselves as Americans and would expect the same to happen with the current waves of immigrants. Furthermore, Greg, the Greek-American, commented to me at one point that race and ethnicity were not always that central to people's lives.

> GREG: By the time I grew up, as the third generation, being Greek was sort of like maybe in a list of one to twenty, being twenty-five. I mean, it was irrelevant. And I didn't feel deprived, because that's not where my source of identity—and I saw it as just, I mean, it was strange Greek stuff coming out when I saw it. . . . I do think there's a kind of Americanization which at the time subtly affects the culture. It's sort of like a historical process that has been going on for three hundred years. And I don't know why it would be any different now.

Native-born white Americans were able to easily shed their ethnicity if they chose to; for current immigrants, there is not necessarily this same choice. However, as some of the staff members saw it, the "optional ethnicity" (Waters 1990, Alba 1990) they are using as white Americans does not need to be any different for immigrants now.

As we can see from the above discussion with Polly, it was not necessarily only the persons of color working at LVEC who recognized the need for diversity among the staff and tutors. Nonetheless, the two women of color, Yolanda and Maggie, appeared to see this need for different reasons than the two white women. The former seemed to recognize that there might be some benefit to the students in seeing others who "look like them" working at the center. Nonetheless, few of the staff I talked with appeared to recognize their roles as Americans, white or not, and the impact that might have on immigrants. One of the few exceptions was a white staff member who said, "I even like being an American they meet, being an ambassador for the country . . . some of the immigrants live in fairly sheltered worlds. They live in a community where they have little contact with Americans." However, she never commented on the fact that she was a white American and what effects this white status might have on the immigrants she encountered.

Cultural agents: Transmitting ideology. The various staff with whom I had discussions perceived their roles in the immigrant community in different capacities. Some recognized their position as often the only English-speaking resource the immigrants had, others simply saw themselves as providing a community base for the immigrants, and still others saw their roles as something of a cultural, American resource. As Greg said with regard to the kind of tutor he looked for: "Wherever they come from is less important per se than who they are and what they do and, you know, that kind of thing. . . . Make sure it's open to anyone who has the desire, willingness, and interest in participating. . . . It's not going to be dominated by any single ethnic group." Additionally, several staff members mentioned the benefits to the volunteers; Bonnie said, "It's just as much volunteers coming together, people understanding and learning from each other." Many of the staff talked about the benefits for the immigrants in having each other to talk to about their positions as immigrants. As Yolanda, a staff member, said, "I think the students rely upon each other in a way sometimes for support." Few, however, seemed to recognize their potential roles as reproducers or challengers of the dominant racial ideology.

One of the few individuals who did talk about such roles was Polly, the native-born white American tutor quoted earlier. She related a story to me about an ESL class she was teaching about neighborhoods in Eastern City. Two students commented that "blacks are responsible for the crime in this city and for their own trouble and their drug use and their property damage" and, further, went on to discuss how, in their experiences, black people were ruder than other people. Polly said she "went ballistic" at hearing this and "tried to unpack those ideas that were packed and they made it personal, so I made it personal." She proceeded to tell me how she explained to them that there were rude people everywhere regardless of race and ethnicity. She said she also talked to them about crime and employment statistics and a recent newspaper article that explored the drug trade as predominantly involving whites from the suburbs entering the city to buy drugs. When I asked Polly why she thought they had this derogatory attitude about black people, she answered, "I don't think people get off a plane, a train, a boat and come to this country and automatically hate people of color." She went on to say,

> POLLY: I think there is some message here that you get early on somewhere, maybe from lots of different places, that people with black skin are to be feared, they're no good, they're lazy, they're impolite, they're rude, they have a great sense of entitlement. You

know, I'm not a scientist but I think that that comes from here. And maybe it fits. Maybe it fits with a longing to belong and blend so that when you get here, even though you think, or you're told, that you're the bottom of the barrel, there's someone you find out that's lower than you are. And that someone is labeled by society. So that pushes you up a little bit, doesn't it? You're standing on the neck of a black person. Then you aren't the bottom of the barrel. And so that's an easy—that's an easy leap, I think.

Here, a tutor used her position to challenge the assumptions of some of her students. Polly, unfortunately, was the exception to the rule. More often than not, I witnessed tutors using the dominant racial ideology of modern racism when expressing their thoughts to their students.

This ideology surfaced most clearly, by far, in discussions of learning English. The tutors and staff continuously expressed to the students the idea that "if you learn English, you, too, can move up the ladder to a higher social class." Here the tutors were inculcating the immigrants with one of the fundamental American ideologies: hard work, such as studying English, will improve anyone's social status. Furthermore, almost every time I observed a class, the tutor would make a point of telling me how impressed he or she was with the students, how hard-working they were, how they often came from two jobs to learn English, and how motivated they were. The tutors' expressions further reinforced the native-born, white-American belief that we live in a meritocracy, where rewards go to those who work hard. As Bonnie, the upper-level white administrator, put it, "[A] lot of them come here [to LVEC] to learn English so they cannot be cleaning toilets."

Furthermore, the tutors and staff worked hard not only to communicate this American Dream ideology, but also to convince the students that race was not important. They did this in two ways. First, they simply did not talk about race, racism, or discrimination in any way; second, they discussed it, but then either minimized it or refuted its existence. For example, one particular classroom exchange I observed was a discussion on affirmative action. The lesson began with the tutor, a white male in his late fifties, asking the students if they knew the term "discrimination"; he concurred when they said it meant "left out." He then went on to ask them if they knew what "race" meant, and when they did not appear to understand it, he explained it as "white, black, yellow, but not something we should be concerned with." When the students asked for the difference between race and ethnicity, the tutor gave examples of white and black Brazilians. Finally, the conversation moved on to the lesson about affirmative action. After explaining the lesson, where an individual (the person's race was indeterminate from the picture) benefits from affirmative action, the tutor asked the students, "Would you mind if a black man got a job instead of you because of affirmative action?" When a Latina student responded that she would not mind, the tutor challenged her by responding, "Really, you wouldn't mind—but they'd be discriminating against you."

In this example, we see the white tutor placing black Americans as "other" against not only himself, but also against the immigrants. Furthermore, as occurs in modern racism, the tutor minimized the importance of race and conflated race and ethnicity. Another white tutor also told his students that race and ethnicity were the same thing. When he asked his students if they knew what "ethnic" meant, a Vietnamese student responded, "Yes, like color of skin." The tutor said, "No, no, like race."

I witnessed other tutors (all white Americans) make seemingly innocuous, yet covertly racist, comments about various racial minority groups. For example, one white tutor talked about gambling with his students and said, "The casinos take money from the economy and don't give anything back, although some of the Indian ones do some good things." In much the same way that the tutor in the earlier example placed himself and the immigrants in contrast to black Americans, I saw another tutor (white, male, and in his mid-sixties) say to the students, "It's not just Americans who speak English—Hispanics speak English also." Here this agent was providing knowledge to the immigrants that promoted the idea of equating "American" with whiteness and furthering the idea that Hispanics are not real Americans. In this class of predominantly Latin American immigrants (out of six students, all but one were Latino), essentially this white American was saying, "You can learn English, but you will still be Hispanic and not American."

Ideology can be thought and ideology can be practice. The agents of this organization are not necessarily openly telling students what to think or what practice to follow, but their words hold power and their beliefs are transmitted by helping to teach the immigrants how to think about race in the United States. Immigrants often have limited contact with other native English speakers, and, therefore, perceive the tutors and administrators as representative of all those who have power and authority in the society. The immigrants acquire the information passed on by their tutors and the staff members and they make it their own.

This knowledge becomes part of their racial habitus and a fundamental piece of the process of racialization. Other pieces to this process are the texts, part of the cultural resources of an organization, with which the immigrants come into contact.

Conclusion

Immigrants learn about the United States, about race, and about their own place in this country in a myriad of ways. They often have little contact with native-born Americans and witness the racial isolation that exists in this country. As Massey and Denton note, "Residential segregation is the institutional apparatus that supports other racially discriminatory processes and binds them together into a coherent and uniquely effective system of racial subordination" (1993:8). New immigrants witness this segregation and the concurrent socioeconomic status and blame black Americans for their place in the US racial and social status hierarchy. Few have said it better than Polly, the tutor I quoted earlier, and it is worth repeating: "So that pushes you up a little bit, doesn't it? You're standing on the neck of a black person. Then you aren't the bottom of the barrel."

More than just witnessing and observing this segregation and the by-products of status, immigrants are specifically being taught about US racial ideologies in the classrooms where they learn English. They are encouraged in their quest for the American Dream, told that little can get in their way if they simply work hard enough, and made to believe we live in a color-blind society. All of these ideas work together to create the modern racism with which we currently live. At times this learning is explicit and specific; at other times, what is missing from the discussions and lessons is what matters.

As I discuss in more detail in the next chapter, the immigrants I interviewed heavily emphasized this modern racism ideology, further reproducing the idea that anyone can make it if they simply try hard enough, that racism does not exist, and that black Americans simply have themselves to blame for whichever socioeconomic status they find themselves in. While this chapter discussed the structural and cultural components to a racial reproduction model, exploring how, where, and from whom immigrants learn about race, Chapter 5 explores how immigrants talk and think about race. This is the expression side to the racial reproduction model.

Notes

1. LVEC is affiliated with Proliteracy Worldwide, a global network of resources working to provide literacy to people everywhere.

2. While many of the tutors had been there for quite some time, there was also some turnover because of the nature of volunteer work. Nevertheless, as we will see shortly, few of the tutors or administrators saw any importance in attempting to achieve a diverse volunteer base.

3. All of the following information is taken from the 2000 edition of LVEC's tutor training workshop manual.

5

Immigrants Express Modern Racism

NOW THAT WE UNDERSTAND SOME OF the ways immigrants learn about race and racism in the United States, as well as their previous conceptions about race in both their home countries and their new host country, we can explore how they express what they have learned. In other words, how is racial knowledge expressed in the words and actions of immigrants? How do they see racial "others" (such as African-Americans and white Americans), what are their understandings and perspectives on race and racism in the United States, and what are their ideas about open social mobility and US achievement ideologies? This chapter, then, is about how immigrants begin to express modern racism; such expression is the beginning of an immigrant's racial habitus.

The Racial Habitus

Habitus, as noted in Chapter 1, refers to socially acquired systems of classification that enable an individual to feel at home in the surrounding environment. Through a person's habitus, we see that individual not as a passive recipient of the beliefs, attitudes, and actions that the dominant group imparts, but as an active agent, interpreting, challenging, resisting, and accepting the dominant ideologies. As Pierre Bourdieu notes, "Social agents will *actively* determine, on the basis of . . . socially and historically constituted categories of perception and appreciation, the situation that determines them" (1992:136, emphasis in original). Nevertheless, Bourdieu recognizes (as Marx did previously) that individuals construct these categories under structural constraints.

While early socialization can have the greatest effect on the development of individuals' habitus, an environmental change (such as immigration) can result in transformation to their habitus. The habitus is constantly subjected to and affected by experiences. The racial habitus immigrants develop derives from immigrants' previous experiences before coming to the United States (including what others told them to expect when they arrived, as well as their previous conceptions of the United States based on media exposure), from the information they receive or do not receive, both before and after coming to the United States, from the various institutions and organizations with which they come into contact, and from the culture surrounding them. The combination of socialization factors—including the media, family and peer influences, organizations and institutions, and agents within these organizations and institutions—is the acquisition side; in other words, this combination helps to construct the habitus. In the previous chapter, we explored how habitus is developed; now, we explore how habitus is expressed.

New members of society must develop a racialized worldview, an understanding of the new society and its racial hierarchy and social structure. This racialized worldview becomes encompassed in the racial habitus, and this racial habitus develops through the racialization process. In essence, the immigrant is "becoming racial"—being encompassed in a racist ideology by acquiring racial knowledge according to the racial constructions in the United States. While many immigrants may already have a racialized worldview that accords with the standards in their home country, they must be resocialized to the host society's racialized worldview. In order to understand this process of developing a racial habitus, we must examine how immigrants speak about race, racism, racial groups/others, and even how they speak about themselves—what is invariably called "race talk" (Bonilla-Silva 2001, 2003, Essed 1991). This chapter then, explores the development of modern racism as expressed by immigrants.

Modern Racism

As explained in Chapter 2, modern racism encompasses several interconnected factors. First is the belief that everyone is treated equally in the United States, regardless of skin color, ethnicity, religion, or any other category. Second, there's the belief that there should be no policies to enforce this color-blindness. Third, and firmly connected to the American Dream ideology, is the belief that anyone who works hard can succeed. Finally, because of the belief that everyone is treated equally and that US society is a meritocracy, the idea exists that people on the bottom of the socioeconomic ladder, primarily racial minorities, are there due to their own cultural deficiencies. The next sections will explore these dimensions to modern racism as expressed by the immigrants in my study.

For these immigrants, these dimensions can be divided into the following categories: first, the idea of abstract liberalism (Bonilla-Silva 2003), which supports the idea of individualism, equal opportunity, and meritocracy. In this case, these ideas are bound together with the American Dream ideology. Additionally, we see the expression that if minorities are not succeeding, it must be through some fault of their own. Second, there's a minimization of the problems of racism and discrimination, and a denial of the very existence of a racial hierarchy. However, as we will discover, what I term the "language leaks" of the immigrants belie this argument. Finally, there is the cultural racism expressed by the interviewed immigrants: the stereotypical terminology regarding other groups, particularly racial minorities, that they consistently articulated. While some of this was spoken in connection with their belief in the American Dream, negative stereotypes were conveyed also in the way they spoke about other racial groups. I will begin with the first tenet—the idea of abstract liberalism.

Abstract Liberalism and the American Dream Ideology

The idea that boundless opportunities exist here, that success is open to anyone who tries hard enough, and that there are unlimited resources for those who do work hard is all part of the American Dream (and modern racism) ideology. This ideology has maintained its stronghold on the immigrant imagination. As Jennifer Hochschild explains (1996), this dream consists of several interconnected tenets. The first is that anyone who wants to can pursue this dream of success. In other words, if one believes in this dream, he or she believes that there are no obstacles blocking anyone from at least trying to attain success. The second tenet is that, if one works hard, then there is every reason to expect that one will succeed in life. Finally, success comes from hard work and no one should expect a hand-out, help from the government, or assistance in any way if it is not deserved.

Immigrants today, just as they have for more than two hundred years, perpetuate this Horatio Alger myth, that with hard work and determination, anyone can make it here. Seeing that some native-born black Americans are in lower-class status positions is at odds with immigrants' beliefs about the United States. For immigrants, if they have fully accepted the American Dream ideology, then there is no other explanation for black Americans' lower socioeconomic status than that they simply have not worked hard enough.

Further, most immigrants believe that if one cannot make it here, then where can one make it? The immigrant chooses to leave his or her home country, often traveling far to try to make a better life in the United States. The idea that the United States is still the "land of opportunity" has not dissipated much in the last two hundred years. Believing in that idea means believing in it for everyone; its corollary is that failure to succeed places the blame squarely on the individuals themselves. Blaming the victims for their poverty status is certainly not unique to white Americans. As one respondent eloquently put it:

> CLAIRE (Jamaican): It's one America [*laughs*]. It's all one America and if you messed up, there's no America you can go, there's one United States. You can go to England or Canada, but everybody want to come to the United States [*laughs*]. Opportunity.

In the following section, I first discuss the different perspectives the immigrants have regarding these ideas of achievement and opportunity. Second, I discuss their own recognition of obstacles to mobility and how they cope with these obstacles.

Belief in abounding opportunities. Regardless of where the immigrants in my study came from, all of them spent a significant time during the interview talking about the benefits of living in the United States and the opportunities that existed for anyone who tried hard enough. I heard respondents repeatedly say that "you can achieve anything you want in America and be anything you want in America."

> CLAIRE (Jamaican): I just want to experience things and I come and it's hard and it's great, you know, because you can make it. You can make it here, a lot of opportunity here if you just keep yourself in the right, in the right hard work.

Later, Claire talked about her own difficulties in Jamaica, being a single mother, and, as she put it, "messing up." In contrast, she perceived endless opportunities in the United States for someone in her position, commenting on the help she had received here as a single mother. For her, the social service system, the public schools, and the government assistance she received were all benefits and resources not available to her in Jamaica. It is worth quoting her at length on this topic.

> CLAIRE (Jamaican): Everybody want to come here because there must be something good here [*laughs*] if everyone wants to come. Because, you know, we can make it here, you know, you can make it here. That's why sometimes I wonder, people who born here and they messed up, everybody going to make mistakes, but they mess up theirself. I wish, oh, I wish I was in that position, I would make the best use. I know I was in Jamaica and I messed up myself anyways, but I think they have better, more than we when I was growing up. . . . 'Cause when you're pregnant, first of all, you can't go back to school and here if you're pregnant they make you go to school and they will help you with the child. There, nobody's going to help you with the child—when I was in Jamaica, I never used to get free stuff. You know, I deal with system here, it doesn't run in the right order. There are better opportunities here. And if you get pregnant when you a young child, you have a social worker, somebody come and sit down with you and talk. There [in Jamaica] is nobody to go and lead you in the right way.

In this way, Claire compared the difficulties she had had in her home country and the help she had received here, then questioned why those who are born here "messed up."

Native-born white Americans often rely on their ancestors' experiences to support the same argument: if one is not succeeding in the United States, he or she must have messed up. This "ethnic myth" (Steinberg 1989) states that this is the "land of milk and honey"; one hundred years later, this myth has not disappeared. Those groups who are thought to have succeeded (however false that idea might be)—the Italians, Jews, and Asians, for example—are seen as the "model minorities." If they could do it, then anyone can. However, as aptly put by Min Zhou and Yang Sao Xiong, "The celebration of the group as a model minority has been politically motivated to buttress the myths that the United States is devoid of racism, according equal opportunity to all, and that those who lag behind do so because of their own poor choices, lack of effort, or an inferior culture" (2005: 1144).

For those in the middle and upper classes, this was often expressed by looking to their own experiences in coming to the United States. For example, Freddy, from Peru, explained that he came from a very poor family and had left school at a young age. Through hard work and determination, he had risen in the ranks of his field, owned his own home, and was able to return to Peru every year to visit family and friends. As he put it, "[A]nd I know that you could do it because I did it." Furthermore, by looking to his own experiences, he, as many of the other respondents, had a difficult time understanding those from his own group who did not succeed or even complained about life here.

> FREDDY: [In Peru,] there's no way you can work as hard as you work here and enjoy life like you do here. Over there you have to work twice as hard if you not one of the big shots over there or belong to one of the big families. . . . Seeing, not only looking at what I'm making now, what I do now, but I look at the future, at what people are making in Lima now, people are my age or younger, by looking at what their future is going to be when they get older, you'd rather die than become old over there. If, if you are middle class or under middle class. But even middle class is, there is, so bad I'd rather die than become old over there.

Not only was it common throughout the interviews for the respondents to talk about the people they knew from their own backgrounds who were not willing to work hard to make it, but they consistently talked about those born here not succeeding through their own fault. For example, although Craig (Colombian) claimed that racism—targeted at Latinos—did exist, he nevertheless asserted, "I think that in this country if you have the qualifications you can achieve anything." As with Claire, Craig did not understand why people who were born here—whites, blacks, Puerto Ricans—"have certain benefits afforded to them, but they don't take advantage of them."

Other respondents used this idea (that anyone can succeed) to further claim discrimination did not exist. For example, Andy (Cuban) insisted, "I think that who wants to succeed can. He who has it in his head that [he]wants to succeed, will succeed. It doesn't matter whether you're Cuban or anything else." I heard a similar argument from Lee, another Jamaican, who claimed, "[A]nybody, from what I learn here in America, anybody can really get somewhere." Later in the interview, Lee echoed the sentiments of Claire, his fellow Jamaican, when he said in earnest:

> LEE (Jamaican): Everywhere, people come from all over the world and get help in America, I mean, that means a lot, you know, when

people out, right now you go every other little place say to the people, "What do you want to do man?" "I wanna to get a trip to
America." Everybody want to go to America, everybody wanna
come to America, everybody come to America and if you have
ambition in America, it's the place where you most, where you
know you have it.

I asked Freddy, from Peru, who placed himself firmly in the middle
class, "So you think anybody, Hispanics, or Asians, or blacks, anybody,
just as long as they're working hard, can succeed?" He answered, "Of
course. I came here with five hundred dollars in my pocket. I didn't
speak the language, I was nineteen years old, and I was not concerned of
how far I have to keep moving or how far I have to go to get to where I
was, but I was happy to look back and see how much I had advanced. . . .
But of course everybody doesn't have that. Lot of people uses prejudices as an excuse." He expressed several times throughout his interview that discrimination not only did not exist, but was used as an
excuse for people who did not want to work hard.

Respondents used stories and experiences of their families and
friends to highlight the possibilities for success in the United States.
Janet (Dominican) used the examples of successful nieces, nephews,
and cousins to explain that anyone could succeed in the United States,
regardless of their race or ethnic background. Andy was asked whether
he or his brother ever experienced any discrimination.

ANDY (Cuban): No, my brother came here with me at the same time.
My brother started as a dishwasher in [the] mall. He worked there
and then he continued to succeed and succeed. Now he's the manager of a mall in Kendall in Miami.

Audrey (Brazilian) also heard about the great opportunities in the
United States from her family. Her aunt told her that the United States
"had a lot of opportunity to get a job and you could make some money
and you had free schools to go to learn English." And when asked what
he had heard about the United States, Jesse said,

JESSE (Mexican): It was beautiful, the US was wonderful, it had
everything and they would tell me it was a beautiful country and
there was opportunity for progress more than anything. Even though
you are small, you say when I grow up I'm going to the US because
they said so many good things about the US.

Here, Jesse shows us the power of the American Dream. It is not difficult to understand this dream in the context of the lives some of the immigrants experienced before immigrating to the United States. For some, poverty and lack of job opportunities in their home countries were the main issues. Janet, living in the poverty-stricken Dominican Republic, heard from others who had been to the United States that there were "a lot of good things, the land of opportunity. Because it is true, here in this country you get a lot of opportunity." Stacy echoed this sentiment:

> STACY (Peruvian): There are employment opportunities, more than in Peru. Here, if you need money and you look for a job, you will find one. If you look for a job as a dishwasher you will find one and get paid. In Peru, sometimes you can't even find that.

This open opportunity in the United States brought many of the more middle- and upper-class immigrants here in the first place. For example, those from European countries talked about the closed systems in their countries and how the structure of the employment systems was much more limiting than it is here. Geraldo was a middle-class professional who had worked in European countries.

> GERALDO (Colombian): The United States has a very open hiring process, which I think is nowhere else that I know of. . . . It's hard to find the kind of openness that exists in the hiring process . . . anywhere else.

For others, often those from Asian countries, coming here was a matter of life and death.

> THERESA (Cambodian): About here, that we, you know, that we not worry about the war, okay, if you work a lot you get money, you have money, you do what you want, you have the law, you know, if you're right, nobody can, like, cheat you or cheat you or something like that. Nobody kill you so easy, if they kill you they gonna find out, it's not like my country. If you work, you get money, then you not worry about someone steal from you, like my country, if you work you worry somebody gonna kill you or rob you or you poor, you gonna worry about you don't have the food for the kid. And you sick, you don't go to hospital or specialty doctor like here, [my sister] all explained about that.

In Theresa's case, it is not difficult to see why she would subscribe so strongly to the American Dream. For some, immigrating was simply a matter of better opportunities and better resources; for others, it was basic survival. Regardless of the reason for immigration, subscribing to the US ideologies that often brings the immigrant here originally means to be in direct opposition to believing in the existence of racism. If racism exists, then it would block that dream's attainment.

Obstacles to the dream. There were very few times any respondents came right out and explicitly said that discrimination or racism would prohibit them from total success in the United States. Instead, they held on tightly to the Horatio Alger story. Nevertheless, they did recognize some obstacles to this attainment; above all, they viewed their struggles with the language as the greatest obstacle to their attaining the American Dream. They repeatedly stated that if they only knew the language better, they would have no problems. Lori, a professional, French immigrant, when asked whether she thought she had a different experience in any way than other immigrants, explained that her English language proficiency put her at a distinct advantage. She talked about an immigrant friend, also from France, who still had not mastered the language completely, and then also noted that the Northern Africans she occasionally interacted with had experienced difficulty because of their lack of language proficiency. When pressed, she maintained that language, and therefore cultural differences, was the only real obstacle for most immigrants to overcome.

Most claims of discrimination also rested on this belief: that the experience had occurred because of the individual's lack of language proficiency. Furthermore, when asked specifically if being their race/nationality/ethnicity (depending on how the immigrant defined himself or herself during the interview) would be a hindrance to success in the United States, time and again the response was, "Not if I can master the language." For example, Theresa (Cambodia) continually focused on language difficulties as the number one problem for Cambodian immigrants. However, she also recognized this as a problem for all immigrants; she recounted a story of a Polish woman in her English classes who had the same trouble. As she said, "[A]ll the people not born here . . . I think they have a problem the same, because it's not the same language. If it's the same language, I don't mind. You can do, I can do, too."

Other immigrants, as the following quotes exemplify, expressed similar issues of language difficulty.

ANDY (Cuban): [Being Hispanic] slows you down because we have to learn the language that is not ours, and that—I believe it slows us a bit.

AUDREY (Brazilian): I think I have the same rights [as everyone]. I could not have the same opportunities because of my English because I am not excellent in English. *{And you believe that if you learn English you can succeed here?}* Yes, I believe that. *{Being Brazilian is not going to hold you back?}* No, it could be a good thing. . . . Because of the language you can speak Portuguese and English language.

LISA (Colombian): I think the progress can be slow, it can be slow, but you can achieve anything you want. *{And what are the biggest obstacles?}* The biggest obstacle is the language.

STACY (Peruvian): The biggest obstacle, I'd say, about being Peruvian here, is being Peruvian here and not knowing the language; that right there is very important.

Some recognized that being an immigrant in itself might hold them back, not necessarily or specifically because of the language, but because, as one respondent put it, "Americans might think we are going to take their jobs away." Or, as Jesse explained it:

JESSE (Mexican): When we are working everything goes well, but when we want to move up, the Americans say no. Sometimes we want to transfer jobs, but they don't let us move up. They just want us to stay there working until the end.

Nevertheless, later in his interview, Jesse insisted that if he knew the language better, he could succeed here. All of the middle- and upper-class immigrants recognized that their mastery of the language would enable them to succeed in this society. While some felt that their accents gave them away as immigrants, they all still believed that they were not discriminated against because they spoke the language so well. Additionally, some of the Spanish-speaking immigrants believed that increased acceptance of Spanish in this country meant that language would not hold their people back in the same way it had in the past. As they correctly pointed out, every major city, and often smaller ones as well, offer information, menus, and entertainment in both Spanish and English. For instance, Geraldo, a Colombian, stated, "I think today you see Spanish everywhere, and you see Hispanic people everywhere. From all over. You can't take two steps without finding someone that looks Hispanic or speaks Spanish."

Because they often felt that this language barrier was their greatest obstacle, believing that their language was becoming more accepted meant that they assumed there were no obstacles at all to their eventual acceptance and success in the United States.

> GERALDO (Colombian): *{Do you think Latino people are discrimi-nated against here in the US?}* [*Pauses*] I think, I think they have been. I think they are being less and less. I think even if they're not openly discriminated against they may be still considered second or whatever. I think the Hispanic community has made great progress in this country. I mean, really has. You know from those days when I came here and couldn't see anybody. Now it's everywhere, you go to the supermarket and everything's in Spanish. Every box you take has Spanish and English. They have become an important part of the social and economic life, the cultural life in this country. Whether you like it or not, that is a fact. And I think one thing that people in this country understand is money. And the more, there's a value not only in the market but also in the products that they offer people, that they produce. The authors, and singers, and musicians, and professionals. They will have to be incorporated.

Some of the respondents did think that people in the United States might have negative impressions of people from their countries, but they rarely felt it had anything to do with their race. Specifically, most of the Colombian respondents mentioned that they feel Americans mistakenly believed that all Colombians were involved with drugs and drug traf-ficking. Nevertheless, they simultaneously believed that most native-born Americans did not know the difference between different Latino groups; therefore, if they did not expressly say where they were from, they did not think this American view of Colombians would affect their lives too significantly.

Even those few immigrants who, on the one hand, seemed to say that there might be some difficulties succeeding in the United States because of their race/ethnicity, on the other hand, appeared to contradict themselves on occasion. For example:

> MANNY (Peruvian): It's a disadvantage to be Hispanic. *{Why?}* Okay, the American, he can assist us, he can service us better because I am

a customer, but he cannot give me the same opportunities to succeed or obtain high positions because I am Hispanic. *{Who is that?}* I am talking about an American citizen, because I ask myself, we have all these Puerto Ricans who have been here for, what, I believe over fifty years. I'm talking about Puerto Ricans as Hispanics, whom I believe have been here over fifty years, and in reference to the Hispanic race, the Puerto Ricans, specifically, they were the first ones to come to this country and I think that they have had enough time to succeed, to have better preponderance in this country. *{But they haven't been able to advance as much as you think they should?}* That's correct. *{And why do you think they haven't advanced more than they have?}* Because, it's true in this country there is a lot of opportunities but only for those who want to succeed.

In this case, Manny at first stated that Hispanics were discriminated against to the point that they were not allowed to succeed, but he then claimed that it was Puerto Ricans' own fault that they had not succeeded in the United States. Later, Manny separated himself, as a Peruvian, from other Hispanics.

MANNY: [Americans consider Peruvians good workers, because] you show up on time, you're responsible, Americans like people who are responsible. They like for you to go to work every day that you are supposed to and for you to be there all the hours that you are supposed to work. It is very important for the Americans, in addition, the versatility of development in any type of work.

Various studies have shown that employers do exhibit preferences in hiring; that they often readily admit that they would rather hire immigrants, or even Latinos in general, than hire native-born workers; specifically, African-Americans (Kirschenman and Neckerman 1991). Interestingly, these employer preconceptions are often replicated among the various races and ethnic groups. Manny was not the only respondent who talked about the lack of hard work on the part of native-born workers. Some respondents pointed to their own group as better workers; others singled out another group. For example, as Freddy (Peruvian) said about Mexicans, "They such a hard working people, you know, good workers . . . that they [employers] felt there was no way they could find here that type of a worker."

Although all of the immigrants talked positively about the United States and were reluctant to speak too negatively about it, some immigrants talked about the false portrait of US life they had received from family or friends.[1] At times, their expectations and visions about the United States were not fulfilled. Several times immigrants spoke about how hard they had to work to get ahead, or even to maintain life's basic necessities. Their comments about this often had to do with the fact that it was not what they had expected, nor was it the picture that their friends or families had painted about the United States.

> STACY (Peruvian): They'd tell me what a marvelous place the US was. Like every country, there are good things and there are bad things. But it's not that marvelous place that Hispanics imagine or South Americans imagine. *{What would they say? Would they tell you about the good and the bad?}* Mostly about the good. The first thing was that you'd be able to come, get a job and earn a certain amount, but they wouldn't tell you how much effort, because over here you have to put in double if not quadruple the effort. They don't mention you might have to lower your standards. The work I do now I would have never done in Peru. It's an honest job, but it's work you have to do. . . . [My aunt] would say—she would try to encourage me to come—she would say, for example, that I could make 350 dollars a week, I would make 1400 a month. She didn't mention anything about the taxes, or how you spend as much as you make. You can earn up to 2,000 dollars, which in Peru is a lot of money, but here it isn't—1,000 dollars is not a big thing.

Stacy's comments are indicative of those of several respondents, who mentioned not being aware of the difficulties they might encounter in the United States. Even so, many continued to believe that the only real obstacle was the language barrier. Even those who did not have the language barrier recognized that they might have some difficulties succeeding in the United States, but still believed that with determination and hard work they could "make it." As Lee, from Jamaica, put it, "I mean you gonna get a little fight in everything you do, from all kinds of people, but at the same time, if you serious about it and move towards what you doing the right way, I don't think, you know, nothing can stop you."

This combination of beliefs—that if they learn the language and work hard and have determination, they will succeed in the United States—helps convince immigrants that their racial or ethnic status will not hold them back. Furthermore, this persistent belief in the overriding American Dream ideology encourages immigrants to believe that racism

does not exist here. This minimization of both racism and a racial hierarchy is the second factor in the modern racism ideology as expressed
by immigrants.

Color-Blind Racism

The immigrants in my study did not completely deny the existence of
racism. Instead, they gave a variety of responses to the question of
whether racism existed and whether they themselves (or friends or family) had experienced any discrimination based on race. Few immigrants
acknowledged the existence of racism, and those who did were predominantly darker-skinned immigrants. Additionally, they justified this
racism greatly whenever they admitted it existed. Therefore, in order to
make clearer the nuances in the color-blind factor of modern racism as
expressed by these immigrants, the next section divides their responses
and expressions into three broad categories that encompass the range of
these ideas and beliefs about discrimination.

First are responses from immigrants who experienced some type of
discrimination, perceived it as racial discrimination, and believed in the
existence of racism. I call this group of responses "racism is alive and
well." However, as we will see, even those immigrants who acknowledged this racism's existence still maintained that it was principally
something expressed by particular groups within the larger society, such
as the police, or perceived it as only experienced on an individual level,
not as systematic or institutional racism. Moreover, those who did argue
that racism exists were usually darker-skinned immigrants, particularly
those from the West Indies. The second group of responses falls into the
category of those not believing in the existence of racism, although they
admitted experiencing some type of discrimination. These respondents
usually explained, or justified, this discrimination as problems with the
language, as simply a mistake, or as something forbidden by the government and, therefore, not as much of a problem as in the past. This group
of expressions I encompass under the heading "racism is dying." The
last set of responses are by those who denied the existence of racism
altogether and, for the most part, claimed never to have experienced discrimination personally nor to have heard from family or friends concerning any difficulties with discrimination. This final group I title
"racism is dead."

Racism is alive and well. Some immigrants expressed the view that
racism did exist in the United States. However, in much the same way

that white Americans often perceive only specific groups, or only certain individuals in a larger organization—such as some police officers—(Tuch and Martin 1997) too, conceived of these groups and individuals as the main sources of racism, as opposed to acknowledging any structural or institutional racism. Or, as Teun van Dijk (1993) explains, white elites often reject overt racism, which they perceive as the only type of racism, and so are then able to exclude themselves as racist producers. In the case of my respondents, there tended to be a similar consensus: the only type of racism the immigrants seemed willing to recognize was overt racism, or blatant expressions of racism.

When I asked a dark-skinned Cuban man in his mid-thirties whether he believed there is discrimination in the United States today, he responded,

> ANDY (Cuban): Yes, I have seen many things. Look at what happened to the African-American, look at what the police did to him. The one in New York. *[Diallo?]* Yes, him and Rodney King. The police. And I also saw another case where the police got only twenty years and they cut a Mexican because of racism. One of them went to court with an American flag, too. If a black person or a Latino would have done that, they probably would have gotten way more time or even a life sentence for doing such a thing.

A Colombian man claimed discrimination and racism exist in the United States; he believed it was aimed at anyone who threatened any of the institutions that were created by whites. However, when pushed for more specific examples, he also located most of the sources of racism in the police, who he claimed stopped anyone who looked Hispanic. A Jamaican man also blamed the police (and the government in general) with racism in his city.

> LEE (Jamaican): I feel that's one of the things why [Eastern City] get so bad because men of law, men of power should handle their job all over the place, not just in the white neighborhood and make sure it's run safe and run straight. I think you demand for the state, the man who run the city, he should, if he handle it—the government handle everything right, handle everybody right, handle everything, you know.

However, later on he rejected the notion that problems of poverty and discrepancies between the wealthy and the poor had anything to do with race. He said, "That don't really have nothing to do with race—anyone on the bottom, just squeeze, squeeze, squeeze, hurt, hurt, hurt." In rejecting institutionalized racism, he located racism as existing only in instances of select individuals, not as a system of larger racial inequality. Instead, he asserted that poverty had little to do with race.

Lee, although not believing class discrepancies were affected by race, did recognize the increasing segregation between white Americans and black Americans.

> LEE: I can notice over the years, I see a big separation, such as whites got to live way down in the woods. The city, they don't—the whites scared to come in the cities, scared to live in this city, and blacks feel the same way, most of them. *{Scared to live in the city?}* No. Scared to live deep in the suburbs with whites.

As a Brazilian woman mentioned, "[B]lack people are in their area and white people in their area, so it's very separate." However, in much the same way that native-born white Americans deny any institutional racism in neighborhood segregation patterns, neither of these individuals saw this segregation as evidence of any larger racial inequities (Massey and Denton 1993).

Other respondents recognized advantages whites received in the United States. A brown-skinned Brazilian woman in her mid-twenties was asked whether there were advantages to being white in the United States.

> AUDREY (Brazilian): I think yes, because of the racism. . . . If you were white you have more benefits than if you were black. If you have black skin. *{Do you think there is any benefit in defining yourself as black?}* Yes, I don't know what, but yes . . . but there is always racism for black people. . . . I don't know why. If they don't like black people, they think black people is like animal, it's not human sometimes and black people don't deserve to be human, to live in here. . . . I've seen it on TV, hear it on the radio, people talking.

Here, she did not necessarily include herself in the category "black," but neither did she include herself in the category "white," equating white with the oppositional term "they."

Similar to Audrey's comment that she had seen racism talked about on television, other immigrants also said that racism must exist because they had seen it on television. For example, respondents would assert that they themselves had neither seen nor heard of any experiences of racism, but that it must exist because it was talked about so frequently in the news or in posters they had seen in government offices. A Dominican woman claimed that racism was much more of an issue here in the United States than in her native Dominican Republic. Asked how she knew it is so much more "marked" (respondent's term) in the United States, she replied,

> ARIEL (Dominican): Because everywhere you go you see signs that states that everyone is entitled to the same opportunities and racism is especially against the law in the US. Because of that and there have been opportunities where a person has felt that they haven't been attended to as they should have. That is racism. . . . It must exist if they have all those signs up. It must be for something.

Jesse, a Mexican man, said that he believed there was a little discrimination in the United States, but it was mostly toward blacks and not other groups. He knew there were problems because he had heard it on the TV news. Again, we see an oppositional categorization: recognizing that racism may exist, but not necessarily for one's own group. Furthermore, the majority of respondents denied that they themselves had seen many examples of racism, but said that they were told it existed here.

Some of the respondents linked the existence of racism or discrimination to specific experiences, whether they encountered it themselves or were told of incidents by a friend or family member. However, of those acknowledging the existence of racism in connection to their own experiences with it, the respondents tended to be darker skinned, usually from the West Indies. Here, a woman talked about her own experiences and how she believed it affected her children:

> ELLEN (Trinidadian): And the kids see how they are treated here. We went to the museum with the kids and when we were there the [white] security guard followed us around, and she yells at the kids for standing too close when the white people in there, many of them were over the black line separating people from the paintings, and our kids, maybe one half a foot over. And then when the kids wanted to use the bathroom she took them downstairs to use a separate one, and then when they were waiting for the bus another guard wouldn't let them wait inside, out of the heat, but they had to wait outside. . . . I looked around. We were the only group all black. Everyone else there was white.[2] [*Shows picture of five kids.*] The

oldest here, is light, and the young one, here, is the darkest. My twins, girls, one is darker than the others. I took them and the boy to school to start on the same day. Then later only the boy and one girl come home with report cards. The other girl, the darker one, with nothing, blank. I call up the teacher and she says, "Well, she wasn't here long enough." And I say, "I brought them all on the same day." And the teacher says, "They can't be twins, one is black."

Here Ellen recounted experiences with racism in two different environments—a public museum and her children's public school. Both times, Ellen felt she and her children were being discriminated against because of their racial classification; she believed her status as a dark-skinned woman from Trinidad made them targets of racism.

Work was a common place respondents experienced any type of discrimination. A Jamaican man and a Jamaican woman also told detailed stories about experiencing discrimination in their workplaces. Lee talked about not receiving respect on the job, about working hard but seeing whites get raises and promotions before him, regardless of seniority. Paula also talked about similar experiences in her office job, where, after her Jamaican mentor and boss left for another job because of her own experiences with discrimination, Paula decided to leave as well because of the lack of respect she was receiving. Others saw discrimination more in their daily lives, such as when they were out shopping or driving around the city in different areas. For example, Laura, a Colombian woman, discussed an experience she had had at a restaurant, where she felt everyone there had stopped talking and stared at her and her Colombian friends.

For this group of respondents, racism does exist, whether or not they experienced it personally. Many claimed they did experience some form of racism; others said that they did not necessarily personally experience it, but they knew it existed based on the experiences of their friends or family, on what they had seen in the media, or on what they had witnessed by the police. However, most of those experiencing racism firsthand were from the West Indies; otherwise, those believing in the existence of racism felt it was not directed at them and located blacks in an oppositional category and as the sole recipients of racism.

Racism is dying. Some respondents believed racism had existed previously, but they relied on the notion that individuals were not legally allowed to discriminate now. By believing, in the same way many native-born whites believed, that racism was eradicated in the 1960s and 1970s and so no longer held any power, these immigrants were able to assert their own ability to ignore racism and deny its power. Here, a man discussed the numerous experiences he had while shopping; claiming that while some whites might treat him poorly, he had the power to ignore them because they were not legally allowed to do so:

MANNY (Peruvian): I feel that I am a very perceptive person. You don't only have to hear what people say but you can tell by the different looks people give you. When you go into a place that is mainly visited by white people you immediately call attention and people turn around and they look at you in a way that says, "Oh, what are you doing in here?" . . . [But] I ignore it and I proceed. I am very conscious that the white person sees me and he might want to be racist against me but they can't do it because legally in this country you can't do that. I know my rights so I just ignore the bad looks. I don't care what people think because they have to give me the same service that they give everyone else. I am very conscious of my rights. I am not going in there to ask any favors, I am going there to solicit a service and I am going to pay for it.

At times, the respondent experienced some type of prejudice or discrimination, yet denied racism existed in any larger, more meaningful way. Andy, the dark-skinned Cuban man mentioned earlier, described having been stopped by the police several times, to the point that he avoided certain areas of the city "known for their white policemen and [where] there are no Hispanics." However, he still claimed that he had never experienced any discrimination personally. Again, later in the interview, Andy described a situation at work where he believed others did not give him respect because he was Hispanic. Yet, when asked outright, he still claimed there was no discrimination in the United States. Janet, a Dominican woman, also claimed that any discrimination that existed was from the police and yet, simultaneously, believed that the discrimination Hispanics experienced was mainly due to language difficulties. As she stated later in her interview, "[Discrimination] is more because of language than because of the race."

At other times, the immigrants were resistant to the idea of any racism existing in the United States, but their experiences belied this reality. Some of the individuals claimed that, yes, they had experienced some discrimination, but they attributed it to the language difficulty, and insisted that all Americans had treated them well. As Jesse, a Mexican man said, "Not racially. Everyone has treated me well. They have all spoken to me well and I can't talk bad about Americans because all of the ones I have found have treated me well."

Above all else, when an immigrant did experience some type of discrimination, or was told of an experience of discrimination by a friend or family member, the explanation would be that there was language "confusion"—the discrimination was based on lack of English language proficiency. Theresa, a Cambodian woman, expressed several times throughout her interview that neither she nor any of her friends or family had experienced any discrimination, but only difficulties because of the language issues. Ariel, a dark-skinned Dominican woman, recounted a story of a friend arrested by mistake, yet explained it away as "a matter of confusion, not discrimination in any way." While the West Indian immigrants were more likely to say discrimination was about race and color, these other immigrants saw the discrimination as being based on language:

> STACY (Peruvian): I don't think it exists, because in the job market, in the opportunities that I have had, had nothing to do with whether I was Peruvian, or Latina, or Hispanic. What affected it, at least in my case, was the language. They could see that I did not master the language and that's what they saw, not because I was Hispanic. I feel that [prejudice] doesn't exist.

> AUDREY (Brazilian): The white American treats Latino or immigrants like they don't know how to speak English. They treat you like they have to speak slowly and you are dumb and the black people sometimes they are interested in something else. . . . I'd meet someone and they think, the white American think because you are Latino you are not as good as them.

All of these examples highlight how these immigrants did not believe discrimination based on race existed; that the only discrimination that existed was based on difficulties with the English language. None of these respondents claimed to ever have experienced any racial discrimination or prejudice here in the United States. Some of the respondents, such as Audrey, were so adamant that racism did not exist that they would provide a clear example of racism, such as being poorly treated because of their skin color or nationality group, and yet, simultaneously, would insist that discrimination did not affect them or simply did not exist.

Racism is dead. The above discussion highlights immigrants who recalled various personal experiences with discrimination, yet then denied the existence of racism and attributed the discrimination to some other cause. However, the majority of the immigrant respondents denied the existence of racism altogether. These immigrants not only claimed never to have been treated in a discriminatory way, but they further insisted that racism did not exist at all in the United States. This racism denial argument existed across different racial and ethnic groups.

Although a majority of the respondents asserting that racism did exist were usually darker-skinned immigrants, particularly those from the West Indies, there were others from this "category" who insisted racism did not exist. For example, Claire, a dark-skinned Jamaican woman, maintained throughout her interview that racism was not an issue. Although she had heard of some people experiencing discrimination, she said, "I never get in contact with no racists. You know, because when people be rude, white people be rude, also black, too, you know be rude." Here, in a similar way to those who did recognize racism, she located racism as an individual case, and a matter of "rudeness," not as systemic and institutional, and not as expressed by any one group in particular. A Dominican woman, who defined herself as a black Hispanic, also claimed there was no longer any prejudice and no benefit to describing oneself as white or black.

Karen, a very-light-skinned Peruvian woman, also said there was no discrimination in the United States, and specifically highlighted blacks as not experiencing discrimination. Additionally, she insisted no benefit acrued to defining oneself as white. Furthermore, although she had been in the United States for approximately two years, she claimed not to know anyone who had experienced any discrimination. Interestingly, Karen said she felt "Anglo-Saxons" did not have a good impression of Hispanics and thought they believed Hispanics were not a benefit to the United States, but in the next sentence she stated, "I don't feel they set limits as to what we can do. I think this country is very open minded, but in reality they don't have a good perception of us."

In asserting that racism did not exist, many immigrants went out of their way to mention how kind Americans always had been to them, and how much they appreciated the openness and acceptance of all groups in the United States. For example, during the focus group that I conducted with four Asian immigrants, none of them acknowledged the existence of racism and said, in regard to discrimination, "It never happens." Furthermore, they took the time to note that they had been treated very well here.

Lisa, a brown-skinned Colombian woman, provides an excellent example of this perception of the United States. Lisa not only insisted that she had never had any experiences with racism, but stated that "Americans always made me feel fine." Additionally, she talked about being warned of racism in the United States when she was still in Colombia, but had never seen any instances of it herself. In addition, she took the time to comment that one of the things she liked so much about this country, one of the "beautiful things you learn in this country," was seeing everyone the same and that "here there is no distinction regarding race." Here, she supported the notion of the United States as a country blind to color, where everyone, in her own words, was treated equally. Lisa's very last comment of the interview underlined her belief; she reiterated, "What I have liked the most about living in this country is that there exists no distinction among the races. Everyone is the same."

This constant expression of color-blindness was expressed by numerous immigrants. Aaron, a light-skinned Cuban man, also made a similar claim that Americans were open and accepting of all groups. He said that not only had he never experienced any type of discrimination, but he went out of his way throughout the interview to mention how helpful Americans had been to him, despite his difficulty with English.

> AARON (Cuban): I haven't had that problem here. I haven't had to confront that problem here because I have never been discriminated against here in this country. Nowhere I have been. Not because I'm Hispanic nor because of my race. I have never been discriminated against. On the contrary, I have received a lot of help because when I first arrived in this country I didn't even know how to ask for water. Today I can ask for even a little more. They have always tried to help and understand me. Because I didn't know the language, I didn't know the idiosyncrasies of this country, it is very difficult to adapt oneself from night to day. But I received help from all of them. What I'm trying to say is that there is no discrimination, they try to help me. . . . I am completely sure that racism does not exist in the US.

Although Aaron claimed that he had always been accepted in the United States, he still placed "Americans" in opposition to himself. He also made a further distinction between being Hispanic (which he saw as an ethnic category) and race, and insisted he never experienced discrimination on either count. Aaron asserted that the Cuban government used the idea of racism's prevalence in the United States as propaganda. He claimed that "[the government] say[s] that blacks are discriminated against here in the US and that is not true. . . . Politics in Cuba are based on saying that there is racism in the US."

Finally, there were some respondents who claimed racism did not exist, but that discrimination could still occur based on poverty. For these immigrants, any discrimination that did happen had more to do with an individual's position in society, regardless of their race, color, or nationality. Geraldo's comments exemplify this argument:

> GERALDO (Colombian): The biggest pockets of poverty are within black America and that needs to change. But things have changed. There's better access for blacks to education, to jobs, to the benefits of the American economy that were not really existent in the 1960s or beginning of the 1960s. *{Why do you think those pockets of poverty exist, then?}* Poverty breeds poverty, and culture, lack of education, and prejudice and people don't really want to put the money where it's needed. . . . *{Do you think it has more to do with class than with race?}* I think it does. I think [*pauses*]. . . . I think the issues for blacks are the same. If you find an educated black, who has a professional degree, who's a professional, who's—he has no problems. Nobody is going to mistreat him or, you know. It's the poverty, really, and the lack of education that puts people in situations where they become the target of discrimination.

The immigrant respondents in this category not only claimed that racism did not exist, but they worked hard to express how positively they had been treated in the United States. Native-born whites have consistently denied the existence of racism, claiming that the United States is a color-blind society, open and welcoming to all groups. Many of my study's respondents, regardless of race or skin color, seemed to support and accept this argument, denying any existence of racial discrimination. However, as the next section explores, often the language they used in the interviews belied this belief in color-blindness and this denial of a racial hierarchy.

Cultural Racism

Expressing ideas about the existence—or nonexistence—of racism is not the only way that immigrants embody their racialization process. We can also see this process occurring through the interviewed immigrants' discussions of other racial groups in the United States, such as their racist remarks about other racial groups and their explanations as to why some succeeded in the United States and others did not. These immigrants often expressed similar views and common stereotypes held by native-born white Americans about various racial minority groups.

In much the same way that native-born white Americans have more recently justified racial inequalities by pointing to the cultural characteristics of blacks themselves as the cause of inequality (Bobo, Kluegel, and Smith 1997), the immigrants I talked with often reflected this same belief.

> MANNY (Peruvian): Black people are discriminated against in this country because they have a different attitude. They have a different way of acting, of behaving. They're uneducated. They believe that they have the right to everything before [Hispanics] do. . . . Black people inside themselves, in their subconscious; they feel that they are being prejudiced against by anyone looking at them.

Others claimed that if anyone did experience discrimination, they must have brought it on themselves.

> AARON (Cuban): I believe that you get treated how you act. If you go into an office and behave appropriately, they cannot treat you inappropriately. You leave your own mark on how you are seen . . . every place has their own rules and these have to be followed. Laws have to be accepted. Any black person can go into whatever restaurant I enter. All he needs is the money to pay for his food. He has no problems at all.

Here, the respondent was essentially arguing that prejudice not only did not exist anymore and native-born black Americans overreacted to supposed prejudice, but that blacks themselves were the source of their own problems. As explained by Lawrence Bobo, James Kluegel, and Ryan Smith, "Rather than constituting a problem widely recognized as justifying ameliorative social intervention, however, these conditions are comfortably accepted, if not in fact actively justified and explained, by many white Americans as a reflection of the choices blacks themselves have made" (1997:20).

Below is a story told by Lori, the professional, middle-class immigrant from France. Lori lived in an urban environment and, believing that maybe she'd made a bad choice about living downtown—having had her car broken into, her bike stolen, a person shot on her street—she described how she saw the black people she encountered in this diverse environment.

> LORI (French): There are lots of black people in my neighborhood and I've never had any problems. Actually, it's funny but there seem to be two communities within the black people that I see or interact with daily. There are all the people who work in all garages and parking lots and there are lots of them around my area, and these people seem to be all from Africa. North Africa, Senegal, and then there are the black Americans who live not necessarily exactly where I live . . . and they come to my area because that's where the bars and nightclubs are and they're very different. 'Cause I interact with the first ones and I don't interact with the second ones. *{Why do you think that is?}* Well, I have no reason to. I interact with the first ones 'cause I park my car and we wave to each other and sometimes we talk if I'm paying my monthly dues. But the other ones I just see because I meet them on the street, but they correspond to the clichés, like the hoods, where they have their hoods on, they're dressed in black. You know, at night they're pretty scary-looking if you think of traditional clichés of gangsters and muggings and, yeah. The grocery store around the corner has this big sign saying "no hoods, no caps" and, you know.

While Lori never explicitly said that the black Americans she saw were causing any problems, she appeared to believe that they were expressing themselves in a dangerous, predatory manner. She clearly, from her description, felt more comfortable with the African immigrants she encountered than with the native-born black Americans.

Interestingly, often the same immigrant who would claim to have experienced discrimination based on race would use cultural racism to explain the situation of blacks in the United States. For example, the woman who earlier recounted in detail how she and her children were discriminated against, now said:

> ELLEN (Trinidadian): At meetings I hear about how black leaders are paid by whites to keep things down. So [black Americans] are fed up and they are scared because when they do fight the leaders tell the drug dealers and then they burn their house down or break their car windows. And for many of them, their kids are the ones selling and doing the drugs so how can they complain about it. It is their own kids. I've complained and people tell me to shut up and I've

had my car windows broken and things thrown at our house, but I always speak up.

During this same interview, Ellen's husband, Doug, commented, "Black Americans are still stuck in slavery and have a low mentality. I have to boss some black Americans and they are angry with me that I am ahead of them. And they are very dumb." Fascinatingly, he then later claimed that racial discrimination by white Americans did exist. A Jamaican woman, who earlier discussed her own experiences with discrimination as well as her Jamaican-American female boss's work experiences with discrimination, made a similar claim: "Blacks here don't care, they make no assertions, don't try to change anything." In the above cases, we have West Indians, or black immigrants, simultaneously arguing that racism existed (as we saw some West Indians said previously) and that it was the blacks' own fault for their placement in the socioeconomic system.

Others claimed that discrimination existed, but still seemed to argue that the lower socioeconomic status of some groups was their own fault. For example, Craig stated that most discrimination took place against Hispanics, and he wondered why because they seemed to achieve success.

CRAIG (Colombian): There is such a poor quality of life in certain communities. For example, in the communities in [a predominantly African-American neighborhood]. . . . From my point of view, people that have been born here and the state provides them with benefits, but people who come from Latin America, be they Puerto Ricans, Nicaraguans, or Panamanians, can become citizens and succeed.

Contradicting what he said earlier, though, he ended this statement by claiming that even the Latin Americans "prefer to stay on the bottom." The idea that blacks are simply not working to achieve upward mobility or respect was repeated for other racial and/or ethnic minority groups historically experiencing racism in the United States. The Peruvian man who asserted that black Americans have a "bad attitude" also argued a similar viewpoint in discussing Puerto Ricans:

MANNY (Peruvian): [Puerto Ricans] haven't taken advantage of the opportunities. They use them to live a life that is too easy because they get assistance from the state, they receive government help. We came here from our culture without any type of assistance from any institution and we didn't have state help, everything we have we had to accomplish on our own, from our own work. It seems to me that Puerto Ricans in this country have it a lot easier than the rest of the Hispanics because they receive all types of help, but they dedicate themselves to use drugs. I do not know any Puerto Rican who has not consumed drugs and this makes me uncomfortable. This bothers me, because I have spoken with a lot of Puerto Ricans and they have no shame. It doesn't even bother them that they haven't studied for a profession. They don't have any desire to reach any goals or to live better, they don't have any interest. They live for the present.

In this case, Manny differentiated among groups of Hispanics; he considered his own group as part of the Hispanic pan-ethnic category, as well as Puerto Ricans, but saw this latter group as not taking advantage of the opportunities he believed they have received.

Another Latino respondent who discussed "bad attitudes" among her own racial/ethnic group was Hilda, an Ecuadorian woman. In response to a question about the problems Latinos might encounter in the United States, she acknowledged that they did encounter some problems, but, simultaneously,

HILDA (Ecuadorian): [They need] not to think that the United States has to bow down to them. Work for what you need. Work for your necessities. Because in our countries the government does not bow down to you. You gotta work hard. As a matter of fact, in my country we never heard of welfare. . . . These teenage girls that go around having babies, and "Here I am, help me"—no.

This stereotyping about racial minorities expecting handouts from the government is a similar view to that often expressed by white Americans, a resentment they have toward black Americans or Latino-Americans, rooted in the belief these groups are receiving undeserved help and assistance from the government. In this way, both Manny and Hilda placed themselves in the same category as Latinos, yet simultaneously distanced themselves from those in this group who they believed were not working hard enough to move ahead in society.

Freddy, from Peru, also expressed anger at the complaining that he heard from some Latinos in this country. During his interview, he talked about listening to a radio show where the announcer had asked callers if they thought this was really the "land of milk and honey." Freddy expressed great dismay at the number of people calling in to complain.

FREDDY (Peruvian): [They say,] "Oh, we come over here and we have to work so hard and in my country I don't have to work so hard," bababa. And, to me, they're narrow minded 'cause there's no way you can work as hard as you work here and enjoy life like you do here. Over there, you have to work twice as hard if you not one of the big shots over there or belong to one of the big families. You have to work twice as hard. . . . Well, for instance, in the radio talk they were saying that, but then I say to myself, they are selfish 'cause they are not thinking about their children or their grandchildren, which in this country their future is open. You know, if you want to be a mechanic you can be a great mechanic 'cause they have the schools for a mechanic. You don't have to go and work under a mechanic for so many years to learn something, you have the schools here. If you want to be a chef, you have schools, you can be a chef. If you want to be a doctor, you have schools, you have plenty of schools to be a doctor. While over there you don't have all that. You have education, you have universities, but I don't believe your options are as wide as here. So for somebody to say, "Oh, I come here and I work hard," like making you feel that they not happy here, well, go back. It's pretty simple. Very simple—go back. And then you're gonna tell me where you'd rather live, here or over there. You know, simple things, for the poor over there, to have hot water, to take a shower and have hot water, they take it for granted over here—a lot of places you have to take showers in very cold water. So they are not gonna tell me, a person, 'cause most of the people that called into the show, they are not highly educated or upper middle class, they are the poor. *{Here?}* Here. I am talking about the Spanish. And I guarantee you, as a poor person here they live twenty times better than the poor over there.

Language

Discourse plays a major role in social reproduction (van Dijk 1985, 1987, 1993). Discourse—including the particular uses of language, the manner in which something is said, and the words chosen—provides us with the ability to explore the interconnections between the individual and the social, between cognition and communication, and between expressions and reproductions of social belief (1993). Although Teun van Dijk focuses on elite discourse, I believe his assertion that this discourse is often implicit, indirect, and subtle is relevant here. Throughout the interviews, I witnessed the rhetorical ploys of positive self-presentation, negative Other-presentation, and, as discussed above, disclaimers and denials of racism (1993).

Language Leaks

At various points throughout the interviews I conducted, I began to see certain patterns of language emerging. For all of the respondents, whether they partially accepted the existence of racism or completely denied its existence, whether they perceived themselves as "color-blind" or not, they still tended to use language that contradicted their initial assertions. I term these contradictions "language leaks."

Above and beyond any other leak in language, I witnessed the continuous expression of Americanness as equating a whiteness status. The immigrants in my study consistently referred to white Americans as simply "Americans," although they always used a qualifier when indicating black Americans. As Joe Feagin aptly explains, "In the United States blackness is usually salient and noted, while whiteness generally goes unmentioned, except when reference is specifically made to white connections to other racial groups" (2000:100). Some immigrants even went so far as to claim that this was a white country, such as Jesse, a Mexican, who stated, "Whites are more ahead in the US since it is their country."

The use of the word "American" to mean "white American" further reinforces white status and the racial system by reproducing the idea that only whites can really be American. The use of the word as an assumption of white status further reinforces the racial system by reproducing the idea that only whites can really be American. Many native-born black Americans claim they are not fully accepted into US society, regardless of their socioeconomic status (Feagin and Sikes 1994), and the immigrants in my study reinforced this lack of acceptance and further contributed to it. The following are just a few examples of the way immigrants used the word "American" to mean white Americans. These are some responses to questions I asked about colleagues:

ANDY (Cuban): Americans. *{White Americans or black Americans?}* White Americans.

AUDREY (Brazilian): Right now, American. *{Black or white?}* White.

LISA (Colombian): Americans. *{Whites? Blacks?}* Whites.

JESSE (Mexican): I also have American friends. *{White Americans, black Americans?}* Whites, of course, whites.

STACY (Peruvian): The majority of my friends are from the church, they are mainly Americans. *{White Americans?}* Yes. . . . There are Americans and there are Puerto Ricans.

Manny used his work experience as a delivery person not only to explain his negative feelings toward blacks, but within this discussion also used the term "American" to equate white.

MANNY (Peruvian): I have worked as a delivery person for Donny's Pizza and when I would go out to deliver something to a black person I would feel this negative attitude towards them. I would go to leave a pizza for an American and they would say, "Oh, I'm sorry because you came out and it was snowing. Thank you for coming out." *{A white American or a black American?}* A white American. But it's not a matter of the amount of tip that they gave you, it's about the attitude. Do you understand? When I would go to leave a pizza for a black person, I would say "good evening" to try to greet them and they wouldn't answer me. Here goes your pizza. They don't say thank you, they don't say anything, and then they don't give you tips.

In this case, not only was Manny expressing his stereotypes about blacks, but he made a clear distinction between blacks and whites, with Americans as the default category for whites.

Janet, a Dominican woman, also qualified her statement when she explained that, although she did not see any difference in how most people were treated, "there are some people, the older generation here, born and raised here, they look at us, Hispanics, like a strange bug. *{Who?}* The older Americans. *{White Americans, black Americans, both?}* White Americans, white Americans." Janet's tone expressed annoyance and irritation that the interviewer did not know she meant white when she said "American." Later in her interview, Janet described an experience she had heard about in which the police arrested a man, in her view simply because he was Hispanic and didn't speak English. She commented that the police were "American police" and, when pressed *{The police were what?}*, she responded, "Americans. *{White Americans, black Americans?}* White, white."

As we will see in the next chapter, the immigrants in my study were not necessarily striving to become white, or even striving to become American, which for them equated whiteness. What they were striving for was success in US society, and they equated this success with white status. Therefore, while they might have acknowledged that they were not white, or Americans, this was the group—white, native-born Americans—against whom they measured themselves. My respondents recognized this tendency to equate Americanness with whiteness, both implicitly and explicitly, and accepted the dominant US ideologies that help to promote this idea.

The final component to a modern racism ideology is the expression of cultural racism: the belief that if blacks are in a lower socioeconomic status, then they are there through some natural or cultural deficiencies of their own. The next section then, discusses the stereotypes these immigrants held about other racial minority groups, as well as their explanations for their beliefs.

Stereotypical Expression

Many of the immigrants were reluctant to acknowledge the existence of racism. While often denying the existence of racism, or even that they themselves saw or cared about race (i.e., claiming to be color-blind to race), all of the respondents would invariably make comments that contradicted this assertion. At times, this incongruity occurred during explanations as to why some people are "at the top" and others are not; sometimes the contradiction was in a justification for an opinion about other groups; and, at other times, the discrepancy existed simply through the language the interviewees chose.

From time to time this contradiction cropped up with those who held positive views of blacks and "others," while simultaneously holding racist beliefs as well. As Feagin (2000) explains in terms of white Americans' attitudes, "It is possible to hold that black Americans can be good entertainers, musicians, or sports figures, yet also believe that most are inferior to whites in character, morality, or intelligence" (125). This seemingly positive, yet racist, viewpoint was expressed by immigrants in my own research. Some of the same respondents who denied that racism was an issue in the United States still asserted that whites were superior to all others in US society.

Some of the immigrants recognized that whites had advantages in US society, but they portrayed those advantages as justified. In response to a question about advantages to identifying as white in the United

States, a Colombian woman said, "[P]eople believe that white people can manage better organizations, and they're more intelligent." Here she separated herself from the belief that whites were superior and, instead, claimed this belief was something other people held. However, in the next exchange, when asked what advantages there might be to having a black racial identity in the United States, she provided a stereotypical response: "Probably in sports. *{So, if you are not playing sports, would it still be beneficial to identify yourself as black?}* If you are going to be a basketball player, for sure. Probably it would be something good." Another immigrant made a very similar comment about blacks as entertainers:

> ANDY (Cuban): When I watch sports and musicians, before they were discriminated against. Now a white person will go near them to ask for an autograph or have a photo taken with them. Now there is paid back. Before blacks were discriminated against. Now blacks are honored, black Americans as well as black Latinos.

Here he seemed to believe that because African-Americans and Latinos are now honored in the entertainment industry, then the existence of discrimination is less of an issue. In this way, blacks were considered superior when it came to entertainment, and whites were perceived as superior in terms of intelligence or management skills. These stereotypical concepts are further exemplified by those who believed this country was founded and is maintained by whites.

Some of the respondents accepted the stereotype that we lived in a "white country," founded and developed by white people. After he claimed there was an advantage to holding a white identity, this man said:

> CRAIG (Colombian): What I see is that since this society originated, since it developed based on Irish immigrants, people from England, who are white skinned, I think, or the idea that I have come to believe is, that they have a more developed idea of what an organized society is like. They were able to consolidate this, they were able to create institutions of power that were beneficial, of people of their same skin.

Others came right out and claimed that whites had an advantage economically in the United States because "a white person knows more about dealing with and investing money" (Jesse, from Mexico). At times, respondents did not limit their understanding of white advantages to a black-white discussion, but would include even their own group. For example, Manny, who is Peruvian and perceived himself as Hispanic, claimed he would rather conduct business in white-owned stores than in Hispanic ones, because "I feel that white people are not going to lie to you, they are not going to try and stiff you and Hispanics will." Although Manny placed himself in opposition to whites by using the word "they," he also held more positive views of whites than he did of his own pan-ethnic group of Hispanics.

Stacy, who insisted that there was no discrimination, gave evidence of her own stereotypical notions of appearance when she attempted to explain how there was no discrimination in the workplace.

> STACY (Peruvian): Let's say my manager, when a black person asks for an application—even if he doesn't look presentable, because their appearance is poor—they receive the same treatment as when a white person who is blond and clean looking applies. He'll sit them down, at least the white one I'm telling you about, he'll sit them down, explain the job and tell them they'll get a call.

Or Theresa, a Cambodian woman, who talked not about her own views but about her family's and friends' views when she said they were "scared of [the city], no go like where all the black people live, something like that, that all my aunts, all the people Cambodia say that . . . scared like, you know, somebody, they scared of everything. Make too much noise and the people no good, because they said in the [city] they sell—all drug dealers, smoke cocaine, something like that." Yet when probed, Theresa said neither she nor anyone she knew had ever had a negative experience with a black person or any other racial minority.

I witnessed another example of the connections some immigrants made between black Americans and crime during an interaction between one of the staff members of the ESL center and a Russian immigrant. This staff member, the only staff person of color, was conducting a language test with this individual by showing her a picture of a darker-skinned man driving a car and asking her to explain in English what she saw. The Russian woman responded that she saw a man who stole a car. Clearly astonished by this response, the staff member probed further, and the woman replied by pointing to his face and saying, "Look at him, he must have stolen the car." Later Yolanda, the staff member, said to me, "Wow, do you think she thought because he was black he was a thief?"

Examples of rhetorical ploys occurred when a respondent made a positive self-presentation and followed it with a negative Other-presentation (van Dijk 1993). Ariel, a Dominican woman, insisted that although she had never seen or experienced racism, it must exist because she saw signs and posters claiming it was illegal to discriminate. She also, however, expressed her stereotypical views about African-Americans:

> ARIEL: Black people are very exaggerated with everything. If they get their nails done, they get a very long one. If they are using something with color, it has to be very bright. If they are going to wear make-up, they make sure it is noticeable. They are more exaggerated than us.

She made this generalized assertion, and therefore generalization, based on her racial habitus.

Finally, as mentioned earlier, it was common for the respondent to explain that black Americans were not relatively successful because of their own lack of hard work. By maintaining this belief, they were then reproducing the stereotype that black Americans are lazy and unworthy.

> FREDDY (Peruvian): When I first came, I happened to train with the, all blacks, they were very dedicated, they were hard-working people, but then the next generation came and it was completely the opposite. Completely the opposite. . . . I have to hire some of them, well, probably about six or seven times, I have people trying to collect unemployment, one was white, the other ones were black. The problem was that they would work, they know how far, how many days or how many months, they have to work before they become eligible for unemployment—the next day, the very next day, you don't see them. They want, they always show up late, the ones that show up, I would say drunk, they want to borrow money in between, before paycheck, but then, if you want to fire them, they gonna destroy your car, they gonna destroy your horses. Lot of times, when I knew I was gonna fire one, I went to them with a gun in my pocket because you never know what their reaction is gonna be. You're firing them cause they are not doing their job, they not showing up on time, they cut corners, yet when you fire them, it is your fault. No, they didn't do anything.

Conclusion

My argument is not that the immigrants I spoke with were necessarily in denial, nor that they were oblivious to some sort of extreme discrimination they were experiencing. I argue that—in much the same way that the majority of native-born white Americans believe that racism is no longer an issue, those who do discriminate are the exception, and that everyone is treated equally regardless of their race—immigrants, too, "buy into" this modern racism. It is one part of their racialized worldview. By first coming here because of their strong and unrelenting belief in the American Dream ideology, and then accepting and expressing the Americanized version of racism, immigrants are truly becoming American.

In the previous chapters, I explored how the immigrants I interviewed came to acquire racial knowledge; in this chapter, I examined their expressions of that racial knowledge. This racial knowledge is encompassed in a racialized worldview in which the immigrant learns the guidelines, rules, and "common sense" notions about race and racism in their new host society. Included in this worldview are not only views on racism, but also the ideologies that accompany modern racism. By grouping the immigrant responses, we saw that the interviewed immigrants fell into three groups: some accepted the idea that racism exists; others claimed racism used to exist, but did not anymore; and a third group completely denied the existence of racism. While they varied in whether they believed US racism existed, the majority of immigrants still expressed ideas reflective of modern racism.

Modern racism relies on some of the fundamental and core (white) "American values": that individualism (not relying on others for help) and hard work will reward you in the end. What I discovered in my research was that the respondent immigrants adhered to these same values expressed by the majority of native-born white Americans. In their initial decisions to come to the United States, believing that they could better themselves by immigrating to this country, they bought into this ideological framework. And by doing so, they accepted modern racism. The various US ideologies are fully encased in a racialized worldview. I argue that it is difficult, if not impossible, for an immigrant to this country to believe that blacks experience any type of discrimination that would limit their access to socioeconomic success. Many of the immigrants work hard, often at several jobs, while simultaneously attempting to learn English; in their view, their struggle must and will lead to success; so, then, native-born black Americans and other groups who are not succeeding are simply not working hard enough.

Nevertheless, there are some hints at challenges to the existing racial ideologies. In the next chapter, I explore how this racial knowledge and racialized worldview help to construct a new identity for the immigrants in their host country. Part of the existing racial knowledge is the persistent view by native-born white Americans that there are only two races: essentially, the white race and the black race. The immigrants in my study challenge this binary construction of race; the majority contend race is much more fluid than this simple, dual construction, and few place themselves solidly in any one category. Therefore, although immigrants are constantly in the process of acquiring racial knowledge, as well as continuously adjusting their racialized worldview, these processes affect the way they see themselves and can allow them to challenge the very system they are learning.

Notes

1. While it is possible that the interviewed immigrants felt obligated to speak positively in front of me, a native-born white American, those immigrants who spoke to my assistant, a Puerto Rican, also were as reluctant to speak negatively about the United States in any way.

2. I later learned the museum she was referring to always provided a docent to a visiting group and maintained a predetermined route through the museum. Additionally, groups were always shown the restrooms on the lower floor, because of their larger space. What we must understand from this account is that it is what is perceived that is important, not necessarily the reality of a situation.

6

Racial Identity Construction

IN PREVIOUS CHAPTERS, I EXPLORED HOW immigrants begin to acquire the modern racism ideology as expressed by native-born Americans. Learning about the racial hierarchy and racial social structure while still in their home countries (from friends and family members who had previously immigrated, as well as through the US media), and then witnessing this racial hierarchy in the form of racial segregation when they arrive, influences their racial habitus. Additionally, they come into contact with native-born Americans who variously express this ideology and influence the racial habitus further. We then were able to see some of the ways this modern racism ideology was expressed by the immigrants: through their color-blind arguments, their cultural racism, and their American Dream beliefs. In this chapter, I am concerned with how immigrants go through the process of racialization—or how the racial ideology they've acquired affects their identification process. I explore how these experiences, attitudes, and beliefs—which comprise their racial knowledge and racialized worldviews—help immigrants construct their identities in this host country.

As I previously discussed, learning about race in the host society is part of the assimilation process for immigrants and their children. The racial social structure affects not only the way they view others, as we saw in the last chapter and will continue to discuss here, but it also affects the way they see themselves. It is in this context that we can see challenges to, as well as acceptance of, the racial system. The primary way the immigrants I talked with challenged the system they entered was by refusing to accept the current binary racial construction. However, as Eduardo Bonilla-Silva and Karen Glover note, when immigrants refuse to identify in racial terms and insist on national descriptors, it helps to hide racial divisions (2004:155). Therefore, while the interviewees might have been challenging the system in some aspect, they were simultaneously helping to reproduce it by accepting the modern racial ideology and making it part of their assimilation process.

This chapter examines the effects race socialization and assimilation processes have on the racial identities of newcomers into a society. Therefore, we examine how the respondents perceived themselves, how they perceived the ways others viewed them, and how they envisioned their own futures. Likewise, we look at the correlation between their racial knowledge, their self-identification, and their interaction with other groups. Both their self-perceptions and the perceptions of others contribute to the reproduction process.

While the immigrants of this study might have wanted to deny the existence of racism in their new host society, and also to deny any connections or similarities to the native-born black Americans they encountered, they still had to contend with the fact that they were not viewed as Americans by the larger host society; they are "forever foreigners" (Tuan 1998). In this way, they will assimilate into their new society, but only to the extent that their racial status will allow.

Southern and Eastern European immigrants in the earlier part of the twentieth century went through a process of racialization, intertwined with class status, that resulted in a white racial identity. Immigrants today, largely composed of people from Asian and Latin American countries, also experience pressure to identify in racial terms; their racial identity is racially distinct from "white," yet ambiguously non-white. They are not white nor black but somewhere in between (Fernandez 2000, Kibria 1996, Lott 1998, Min and Kim 1999, Palumbo-Liu 1999, Piatt 1997). The ongoing interracial tensions we see in society today are in part due to this racial ambiguity, which arises out of one's different racial and class positions and one's quest for preferred and privileged status in a racial hierarchy.

Racial Ambiguity: Who Am I in a Racialized Society?

A great deal of confusion and disagreement exist over the terms "race" and "ethnicity." However, I argue here, in accordance with the point made above by Bonilla-Silva and Glover (2004), that any denial of a racial classification is part of the racialization process. The immigrants I worked with had begun to encompass the modern racism ideology into their racial habitus; as such, this modern racism ideology affected their identities. If they believed that black Americans were in a lower socioeconomic position because of their own deficiencies, then they must distinguish themselves from this racial group. Further, by refusing to accept a racial marker, the immigrants were denying the importance of race and their places in the racial hierarchy. If they claimed they did not have a racial identity, that goes along with their modern racism ideology, which holds that race is not an issue (color-blind racism).

I began exploring the question of the immigrant respondents' identities by asking them to think about the census form's questions on race and ethnicity and decide how they would answer these questions were they filling out the form for themselves. The form asks the respondent what his or her race is and then provides the following options: white; black/African-American/or Negro; American Indian/Alaska Native; Asian or Pacific Islander (Asian Indian, Chinese, Filipino, Japanese, Korean, Vietnamese, Native Hawaiian, Guamanian or Chamorro, or Samoan), as well as "other Asian or Pacific Islander"; and a final category of "some other race." Additionally, for the first time, the form allows individuals to choose more than one race category. In terms of ethnicity, the only question on the census form is whether the individual is Hispanic, Spanish, or Latino. If yes, the following options are available: Mexican/Mexican-American/Chicano; Puerto Rican; Cuban; "other Spanish/Hispanic/Latino."

The majority of the respondents were surprised by the census form's division of racial categories. If we look back to Chapter 3's discussion of how race and ethnicity have traditionally been defined in most of the immigrants' home countries, we see more of an emphasis on nationality groups or geographic groups. But the most striking idea that came out of almost every interview was that race was really about color. For these immigrants, race was not a politically defined category, such as it might be for native-born citizens of the United States; instead, when asked about their race, or even other people's races, the majority of the respondents answered in terms of color. This response was particularly evident when the respondents answered questions about their views on who was characterized under the term "person of color." For some respondents, an Asian person was considered a person of color; for others, only native-born black Americans were considered persons of color.

At various points, immigrants would insist that there was simply no distinction between race and ethnicity, particularly if they only saw race as color. For example, when I asked Manny, from Peru, what he would check off for his ethnicity, he proudly stated, "Hispanic!" When I asked what he would check off in reference to his race, he again responded,

"Hispanic." After I showed him the choices provided on the form, he then said he would simply write in "None." Manny's response was similar to that of many of the Hispanic respondents of the census; they were not a race as defined by the census categories, they were simply Hispanic (Rodriguez 2000:130). Stacy, also from Peru, did not feel comfortable choosing any of the options for the race categories and, instead, said she would put down "other." She also claimed that Latino should not be considered a racial category, because "it's a group of people that really do not have the same race, not necessarily." As she explained it, her perception was that the word "Latino" referred to people from the same geographic location. Laura, Colombian, continued to insist throughout her interview that the only response she would have for race was "Latina." As she said, "There are a lot of us who do not identify ourselves with the options that they give us." When I asked whom she meant by "they," she said, "Americans."

Some of the Asians I spoke with also conceived of race as being about color, with ethnicity referring to either national identity or a pan-ethnic category. During the focus group I conducted with four Asian adults—one from Cambodia, one from China, and two from Vietnam—when I asked about the different races of those in the room, the respondents defined race in terms of color. Sam, a very-dark-skinned Cambodian man, pointed to both the Chinese woman (who was very light skinned) and me as being white, yet simultaneously saw himself as Asian-American. This "color distinction" between race and ethnicity is consistent with Nazli Kibria's analysis that an ambiguous racial identity exists for South Asians (1996).

The situation for the European immigrants I interviewed or spoke with was very different from the experiences of the Asian or Latino immigrants. Both Franny and Patty, the former from Italy and the latter from England, commented on their whiteness status, but would quickly mention they were not American, either. Neither of these women perceived themselves as members of a larger pan-ethnic category, such as European-Americans, although Patty had been living in the United States for twenty years, off and on. Franny saw herself as being in "limbo," not American and not Italian. Lori, from France, saw herself as only and always French, although she had been in the United States for approximately ten years. She, too, said she did not see herself as white, although she did concede that others would likely see her that way. For the European immigrants, their racial status was not nearly as ambiguous as it was for other immigrant groups. Nevertheless, it was interesting that one of the European immigrants I spoke to, who was from

Spain, definitely identified herself as a member of the Latino ethnic group. To her (Pamela), it was the Spanish language that united Latinos, not the geographical location from which they come.

The following discussion explores the various ways the immigrant interviewees spoke about their own identity, and how they separated themselves from native-born Americans, both black and white.

Self-Identity

Other scholars have explored the various factors that are likely to affect the racial identification of immigrants (Golash-Boza 2006, Portes and Rumbaut 2001). Looking specifically at Latinos, Tanya Golash-Boza determined that discrimination and exclusion have a direct result on the identification process. She contends that "those Hispanics who do experience discrimination are less likely to self-identify as American because the discrimination increases their awareness of their non-white status in the United States" (29). She goes on to argue that these same individuals are more likely to self-identify as Hispanic because of the discrimination they experience. Alejandro Portes and Ruben Rumbuat further explore these questions with regard to the second generation; in this case, they also find a relationship with discrimination. As they state, "Two-thirds of those who defined their race in pan-national (Latino, Hispanic, Asian) or exclusively national terms had endured discrimination" (181). The connection between discrimination and identification is obviously a crucial one. What is interesting here, though, is how the identification these respondents chose was not necessarily a racial one, regardless of their experiences of discrimination. Choosing a national or pan-national identification is still a way to distinguish oneself from those on the lower end of the racial hierarchy. These immigrants and their children might not have seen themselves as white, or American, but they were also not being perceived as black.

Race is about color. While these immigrants might have rejected racial labels because of their insistence on separation from black Americans, another reason could be that they only saw race as a question of color. The Latino immigrants, in particular, provided a variety of responses in terms of their own "color"; some answered "White" to the question about race, others answered "Black," some filled in the category "Other" with the term "Mixed," and some insisted that "Latino" was their response to this question. These responses were consistent with recent information from the 2000 US census survey, where about 43 percent of Hispanics or Latinos classified themselves as "Some Other Race"; and of *all* people who reported "Some Other Race," 97 percent were Hispanic or Latino.

By comparing some of the responses of Latinos and, more specifically, of individuals from the same country, we see further examples of how race has more to do with color than with social or political categories. Lisa, a Colombian woman, defined herself in racial terms as white, and said she should not be considered a person of color. She also did not believe that Latinos in general should be considered persons of color, regardless of their skin color. Craig, another Colombian, while simultaneously saying it would be difficult to choose one race category for himself, did end up identifying himself as "somewhat white." Furthermore, he believed that Hispanics could be defined as persons of color. Nevertheless, he claimed that in the United States, when anyone referred to a person of color, they were referring to a black person. He also said that he knew Hispanics who had gotten into trouble, such as arguments with native-born black Americans, for using the term "person of color" in reference to themselves in the United States, because in this country it should only be used in reference to a black American.

Karen, a light-skinned woman from Peru, claimed not to be a person of color, and only conceived of black Americans as persons of color as long as they were "very, very black, in regards to color, and born here." She talked about her parents in a similar way: "My mother is white, white, white and my father is not black, but is very dark. My father is very, very dark, but not black. He is dark skinned." Karen wanted to make it very clear that there was a distinction between being a dark-skinned Peruvian and being black. She clearly did not want to be part of this group ("persons of color"), nor did she want her father considered a part of this racial category. Later in the interview, she said, "[Since] I am neither black nor Chinese, I am white." Most interesting was that all of these respondents denied the existence of racism or discrimination against black Americans. Thus, on the one hand, they might have recognized the category "persons of color" as specific to black Americans— and as a category they did not want to be in—but, on the other hand, they did not believe there was any racial discrimination based on this categorization.

For the darker-skinned immigrants, we might have expected to see more connections to black Americans in both experience and identity. As we witnessed in the previous chapter, though, even those immigrants (who might be categorized as "black" by native-born Americans) often did not believe racism was a significant problem, and continued to make distinctions between themselves and these native-born Americans. For example, Andy, a dark-skinned Cuban man, did define himself as a person of color, including himself in the category "black," yet clearly distinguishing between black Americans and black Latinos. Throughout his interview, Andy made distinctions between "black Americans" and "black Latinos," calling himself a "black Cuban." As we saw in the previous chapter, Aaron, a lighter-skinned Cuban man, did not believe in the existence of any forms of discrimination in the United States, while Andy did believe that some forms existed, specifically with regard to the police. When we consider that Andy, dark skinned, said he was stopped by the police and watched more closely, we can begin to understand why he might have identified as a person of color, while his compatriot, Aaron, light skinned, did not.

Audrey, a medium-brown-skinned Brazilian woman, showed the confusion general to many respondents. She said that a black person was a person of color and if Latinos were dark skinned, they, too, were persons of color; further, she considered herself a person of color, but she would check off the "Other" category for race for herself. She explained that she would check off this category because she was not black like black Americans. As we will see below, this sense of confusion often came from how others categorized the individual, which, in turn, changed how they saw themselves. Audrey appeared to reflect the views of many of the respondents when she said, "In the US, I'm confused."

Me vs. native-born black Americans. For West Indians, there is no doubt that they view themselves as black; however, again, this "blackness" is as a black immigrant, not as a black American (Duany 1998, Foner 1998, Vickerman 1999, Waters 1999). As Nancy Foner says, "West Indians strive to differentiate themselves from African-Americans and show the white majority that they deserve to be viewed as superior and granted respect" (180). However, many scholars focus specifically on black immigrants (e.g., Jamaicans) who also would not view themselves as part of the pan-ethnic category "Latino," which is not necessarily the case for some Dominicans or Cubans. Some immigrants from the Dominican Republic adopt a Latino identity, which then also serves as a form of racial identification (Bailey 2006, Iszigsohn and Cabral 2000).

Ariel and Janet, both dark-skinned women from the Dominican Republic, identified racially as black and ethnically as Hispanic. However, they both were clear on distinguishing themselves from native black Americans.

JANET: For me, I'd be of the black race. *{So you'd identify yourself as belonging to the black race?}* Well, here the black race is a different thing. You see? Here in this country the black race are Africans or Jamaicans. I cannot classify myself like them because I have no knowledge of either Africa or Jamaica. But I am not going to classify myself as white, either. In regards to group, Hispanic.

Here, Janet not only distinguished herself from black Americans, but she also did not necessarily consider herself in the same category as black immigrants, either. Neither of these women, although identifying as black racially, conceived of racism as a current issue in the United States.

Jamaican respondents also were clear in what they saw as distinctions between themselves and black Americans. For example, Paula was very unambiguous in talking about what she thought her son's identity would be, saying, "[H]e's black . . . [but] he's not African-American, so they better not call him that." In this case, "they" again referred to white Americans, whom she did not want confusing her son with native-born black Americans. Nonetheless, Claire, also from Jamaica, said she would consider herself black, and if she were asked specifically, she would say "Jamaican black," but otherwise, "just black." And although Ellen and her husband, from Trinidad, had been in the United States for many years and had worked in several community groups with native-born black Americans, she distinguished herself from these black Americans, while simultaneously recognizing her racial association with them. As she said, "Black American leaders don't do anything for blacks or West Indians." And as Doug, her husband, pointed out, "We all might be black skin color inside, [but] West Indians are different, different culture."

Some of the West Indian respondents distinguished themselves from African-Americans during their discussions of the existence of discrimination. Even though they might have acknowledged the existence of racial discrimination against themselves, at times they also claimed that if blacks were not succeeding or if they were experiencing trouble, they had only themselves to blame. By believing that this was the land of opportunity, that anyone could succeed who worked hard enough, and that black Americans did not take advantage of these opportunities, black immigrants insisted on separating themselves from black native-born Americans.

Pan-ethnicity. As previously discussed, one of the ways immigrants choose to identify in their new host society is by the use of pan-ethnic labels. This is actually the most common form of identification, particularly among those who do not identify racially. Often, immigrants will use both their national identification (to distinguish themselves from others in their pan-ethnic group) and a pan-ethnic identity (to distinguish themselves from other racial and ethnic groups).

In speaking about pan-ethnicity, most authors tend to focus on how groups are defined as one larger category by those not within the group (Espiritu 1992, Winant 1994). For example, some authors have looked at how individuals from various Asian countries are lumped together with all Asians, regardless of their ancestry, so that instead of being perceived as Japanese-American, for instance, they are seen as simply Asian-American (Tuan 1998). My respondents tended to see similarities with other immigrants in their pan-ethnic category and more differences between themselves and native-born Americans, from both different ancestries and the same national backgrounds. For example, Theresa spent a considerable part of her interview talking about the differences between herself, having arrived in the United States in 1997, and those in her family who were raised here.

> THERESA (Cambodian): I can feel like the Cambodian, about the way they wear, depend on the Cambodian, they was born here, they, you know, like they born here mean they not like the Cambodian from the Cambodia. . . . Okay, like wear the clothes show or something too tight, that the way the Cambodian culture—they do that because all the culture we never see the skin at all for women. They wear long, turtleneck long, that the culture, Cambodia, Thai, Lao, the same culture. We have the New Year the same day, everything culture only different a little little bit. . . . I saw my cousin, my sister-in-law, she was, only the way she act, the way she talk, she not Cambodian, that mean I say that. I say if Cambodian grow up here I have no idea but the way they talk, the way they act, the way they wear, it's not the Cambodian. Different. . . . *{What is it?}* But the face, the body, that Cambodian, but they are the mind, they are the opinion, it's not Cambodian. *{So what is it? If it's not Cambodian, is it . . . Asian? Is it American?}* American. *{American?}* American [*more firmly*].

Theresa said that, in general, she felt more similarity between herself and other Cambodian-born immigrants than with Cambodians living in the United States. For her, these other Cambodians were well on their way to being Americanized, a style to which she did not feel she could relate. This is a common refrain among immigrants, as we will see in the section on their children's identities; the immigrants often struggled to maintain some part of their ethnic identities, for themselves and their children.

While Theresa mentioned that she did not resent the pan-ethnic category "Asian," if that is what native-born Americans chose to call her, other respondents resented the classifications that grouped them with others from similar backgrounds. For example, Ellen, from Trinidad, continuously mentioned herself as a West Indian, and said that is how she filled out the census. However, she also mentioned several times that she did not like the assumptions that all West Indians were from Jamaica, and she resented the grouping. When I asked her whether she would be attending the West Indian parade in the local city, she responded,

> ELLEN (Trinidadian): No, that is not really a West Indian thing. . . . These programs will say "West Indian," but really it is just for the Jamaicans. I took the kids to a program at the West Indian club and everything was about Jamaica. All the balloons on the tables were their colors and the posters and everything. There's more than just Jamaicans here.

It is also interesting, though, that throughout her interview, Ellen talked about herself as West Indian, whereas the three Jamaican respondents always referred to themselves as Jamaican, not as West Indian. For the Jamaicans, being part of one of the larger West Indian groups in the United States (especially in the Northeast, where this study took place), there was not as much necessity to identify as West Indian. For Trinidadians, there was a greater need, in terms of resources, political power, and status, to define oneself as part of the larger pan-ethnic category.

Almost all of those from Latin American countries considered themselves part of the larger pan-ethnic category, "Hispanics," or "Latinos." However, although they seemed to have no misgivings about using either category to describe themselves, many still tended to locate their identity within their own nationality groups, such as Colombian, Brazilian, or Cuban. Lisa, for example, said that "Colombians are Hispanic," but that she would describe herself as Colombian. Or Andy, who said, "I'd identify myself as Latino, no matter the color or the race, Latino," but also said that once he received his citizenship, he would identify as Cuban-American. Manny, from Peru, showed how, on the one hand, a Latin American immigrant might accept this pan-ethnic category, saying he saw himself as Hispanic, but, on the other hand, did not necessarily want to be lumped together with all the others in that category. He said, "I would like to be identified as Peruvian and I don't want them to generalize me with any other group of Hispanics." This reticence to identify with a pan-ethnic group could, at times, be reflective of the stereotypical views one might hold about the group, as we saw evidenced by Manny and Hilda (Ecuador), who both spoke derogatorily about Hispanics.

Others did not necessarily continue to use their nationality group to identify themselves, but instead relied on the category "Latino" more readily. For Laura, from Colombia, "Being Latina is what describes me"; she said she would simply respond "Latina" if someone asked her "what she is." Craig, also from Colombia, felt very proud to be Latino and identify as such. As he explained it, "Latino is that person that shares a tradition, a culture, and a same language . . . but more than language, there is more to it than language, it's the point of view that there is a way to look at life, the way that culture is appreciated."

There were, however, some immigrants from Latin American countries who did not locate themselves within this pan-ethnic category. For example, Audrey, from Brazil, responded to the question of what she said when people asked her "What are you?": "'Latino'—no, I don't say 'Latino,' I say 'Immigrant,' 'Brazilian.'" Jesse, from Mexico, never once used the term "Latino," only "Mexican."

It is quite possible that, over time, many of the immigrants who now do not refer to themselves as members of a larger pan-ethnic group may do so (Espiritu 1992). The majority of immigrants I interviewed were relatively new to the United States. Over time, identifying as Latino or Hispanic versus Brazilian or Mexican may seem like a more beneficial option. Political and social power often come from numbers; some of these immigrants might begin to realize that identifying as part of the larger group would reap greater rewards. Some of the more professional and highly educated immigrants recognized this advantage, arguing, as did Geraldo, from Colombia, that Latinos had power in numbers, and identifying as such would be the only way they could succeed in this society.

Future identity: To hyphenate or not. As Mary Waters (1990) explains, white Americans with European ancestry have essentially two options: they can choose to be white, with no ethnic identification, or they can choose one of their ancestral backgrounds to hyphenate with "American." Because of their position as the majority group within the

United States, whites have the power of this "optional ethnicity." More recent immigrants—those from Latino, Asian, and West Indian backgrounds—do not necessarily have this same option, nor do they necessarily want to be "American" hyphenated at all. Again, we see this identity construction as related to the perception of others around them in society; as Jorge Duany says, with relation to Dominicans in the United States: "The persistence of a Dominican identity in the U.S. may be interpreted in part as resistance to the prevailing racial order" (1998:166). It is possible, then, that immigrants who refuse to accept the hierarchical racial order for themselves are making challenges to it by continuing to use a national identifier. However, it is also possible to interpret this as a way to insist that race does not matter in the United States.

Immigrant respondents varied greatly with regard to identifying as simply their own nationality group or as a "hyphenated American" group once they received their citizenship. For some, there was no way they could ever see themselves as identifying as an American (hyphenated or not), while others believed that receiving their citizenship would automatically mean they would adopt a hyphenation. At times, the choices appeared to be related to the respondents' levels of feeling accepted in US society; at other times it had to do with their desire or willingness to become American (depending on what that meant to them); and, at some other times, it was simply a matter of clinging to their national identification.

Although I did not compare race or ethnic identification options with regard to the factor of age, some might argue that the decision to hyphenate could be related to either the immigrant's age of immigration or the immigrant's time spent in the United States. However, a brief examination informs us that age did not necessarily have an effect on this issue, with some older respondents believing they would add "American," as part of a hyphenation, to their identity, and some younger respondents claiming they could never foresee this possibility. Importantly, regardless of their beliefs about hyphenation, none of the respondents claimed that they would ever be simply American. For instance, when I asked Theresa whether she thought that at any time in the future she would call herself "American" or if she would always be solely "Cambodian," she replied, "No. *{No, what?}* Because the way I am, the way I look that the Cambodian, I never think, 'Oh, I'm the white skin.' I cannot say that." For Theresa, as for many of the other respondents, white status was equated with American status, even though previously she had stated that her Cambodian relatives who were born here were "really Americans." For her, not considering herself as white, she believed there was no way she would ever be truly American. Ariel, from the Dominican Republic, also did not see herself as ever using "American" as part of her identification. When I asked how she current-ly identified herself, she replied,

> ARIEL: Hispanic. *{Hispanic. What will you say in five years?}* Hispanic also. *{What about if you dominate the language and are here a longer period of time, what are you?}* Hispanic. *{Do you think you will ever add the word "American," "Hispanic-American," to your classification?}* No, because in reality I am not American. *{If you obtain your citizenship and dominate the language, you will not change your classification?}* Never.

Similarly to Ariel, Audrey, from Brazil, said that regardless of her citizenship status or her length of time in the United States, she would always remain Brazilian. We can see in these cases how age did not seem to affect this decision, as Ariel was in her thirties, Audrey in her twenties, and Aaron, from Cuba, in his seventies. Aaron also believed that regardless of whether he received his citizenship, he would always remain Cuban. As he said,

> AARON: Well, your roots are never lost. Even if I was to become a US citizen, I would never lose my roots. I would be a US citizen, but a native of Cuba. That means that I would have roots from both places. *{If someday you obtain your US citizenship and I ask you "What are you?" what will you say?}* Cuban.

Other immigrants, like Aaron, felt very strongly that this national identi-ty would never change. As Manny explained it,

> MANNY: The term "Peruvian-American" I cannot conceive. I don't see any use for it at all or see what it's for. I can tell you that I can be here thirty years, but when you enter my house it is going to be as if you are entering a small part of Peru. What I want—and I want to maintain this tradition. Maintaining the culture, it is that formation that we have in our families that they give us in our countries. No one is going to take that away from me and I am going to make sure that my family, that my future family and my children know this.

For some of the immigrants, receiving their citizenship was the barometer for choosing this hyphenated identity. For example, for Stacy, from Peru, simply receiving her citizenship would make her Peruvian-American, but until then, she would identify as Peruvian. She stopped, however, at saying she would ever consider herself just American. Or Andy, who is Cuban, who believed he was "in the process" (his words) of becoming Cuban-American.

> ANDY: I will identify myself as Cuban-American. Yes, I would add "American" because that's a commitment I would have made. That is an oath I would have made, but I wouldn't take the "Cuban" out to just say "American."

Jesse made a similar point when he said that receiving his citizenship papers would make him American, but, "I will always be Mexican."

For the respondents who believed they would adopt a hyphenated identity, acceptance of "American" as part of their identification was largely related to attaining their US citizenship. There were very few respondents who believed they would ever drop their national classifications from their identities and identify as simply Americans. Claire, from Jamaica, who identified as black racially, also said she would like to hyphenate her identity. Claire was one of the few respondents saying she would, because of her racial identification, perceive herself as part of the larger pan-ethnic group: black American. As she stated, "I would say, I know, I—that I didn't born here but I'm here, so I would like to consider myself as the same as, you know. . . . *[So, if somebody asks you what you are?]* Black American." Even Ellen, also from the West Indies and who had been in the United States much longer than Claire, did not see herself as ever identifying as solely black American.

Children's Identities

The previous wave of immigrants desired that their children become Americans and yet retain some of the old-world ways. As they successfully assimilated and became Americanized, it became more acceptable to become hyphenated Americans. Despite the discrimination in the early 1900s against Irish, Italians, and Jews, it has now become fashionable to be Irish-American, Italian-American, or Jewish-American (Waters 1990). The children, grandchildren, and great-grandchildren of these earlier groups of immigrants take pride in their ethnic identities and seek to hold onto their parents' foods, traditions, and cultural identities.

Today, the story may be very different. As discussed in Chapter 2, this current wave of immigrants is not necessarily going to be afforded the same opportunities for assimilation as the earlier wave. Instead, as Portes and Rumbuat identified, the children and grandchildren of this current group of immigrants are more likely to experience a segmented assimilation (2001). The authors correctly cite several factors that can affect this assimilation process, such as family, community, and economic resources; however, they have a limited discussion of the effects of racism and entering this racial context not only on the assimilation process, but also on the identity of the first and second generations. While my work here focuses on the first generation, it would certainly be worthwhile to further explore the effects of the larger racial context and racial knowledge acquisition on this second generation. My respondents could only surmise what identities they believed their children would adopt.

While there were differences among the immigrant interviewees concerning their own future identities (in terms of whether they would hyphenate their identification with the qualifier "American"), almost all of the respondents believed their children's identities would be hyphenated. This hyphenation did not necessarily depend on whether the child was born here, but had more to do with the respondent's desire for the child to retain elements of the parent's home culture as well as to recognize his or her new identity as an American. For example, Lisa (Colombian) saw herself and her son as racially white, but whereas she could not see herself adopting "American" into her identification, she did see her son as either "Colombian-American, or American-Colombian."

Instilling in their children pride in their home countries was clearly very important to most of the respondents, regardless of whether their children were born in the United States or not. As Craig said, his son would be "Colombian-American, and we will try to instill in him a lot of our culture and our values. But we also acknowledge that he is also going to acquire certain American values." Craig, like Lisa, claimed he would never adopt an American identity, and said he would always simply be Colombian, or a Colombian with US citizenship. Those respondents who recognized that their children would likely adopt this hyphenation, while they themselves chose not to, placed themselves in opposition to their children. However reluctantly, they recognized their children would be partly American.

Others who identified with a pan-ethnic classification also saw their children adopting this same identity, such as Hispanic-American, or, like

Claire (Jamaican), as black American. Janet, from the Dominican Republic, believed her children would adopt both the identity "Hispanic-American" as well as simply "American." Stacy, while seeing herself as Peruvian-American once she attained her citizenship, also imagined her daughter using this identity, but said that she would want to continue to "emphasize to her that she is Peruvian-American because her country of origin is Peru."

Some immigrants, however, were comfortable with their children's taking on the unhyphenated identity "American." Audrey, while claiming she would always only identify as Brazilian, saw her US-born children as simply American. Theresa, who noted distinctions between those Cambodians born in the United States and those who immigrated to the United States, also felt her children were not necessarily Cambodian.

> THERESA: I never think they be like the Cambodia because they grow up here, they born here. . . . But the way they look, that mean they the Cambodian, they the Asian, but the way they act, the way they talk, I don't know, but I think that—my opinion, think they not like the Cambodian, they never think like that.

Regardless of how immigrants envisioned their own future identities, all believed their children would take on an American identity, either hyphenated or just American. None, however, wanted their children to lose their parents' nationality ties, and all expected their children to recognize "where they came from." Theresa provided a good example of how, at the same time, most of the immigrants recognized that their children would feel differently from them, because they either were born in the United States or grew up in the United States.

This adoption of an American identity for their children indicates another potential challenge to the racial classifications and hierarchy existent in the United States. In previous chapters we explored how the majority of immigrants viewed American as equating whiteness status; by believing their children might one day also acquire this marker, they were then believing that their children would be accepted into the larger, dominant white society. Nevertheless, by continuing to expect their children to use the qualifier of their home country in the hyphenated identity, they are simultaneously saying their children are not "full" Americans. Does this mean, then, that the immigrants and their children can never truly be defined as American, and only native-born white Americans can be?

Being Defined and Doing the Defining

Defining Oneself

Many minorities in the United States, such as Asian-Americans, are still separated by the cultural and racial boundaries within the United States, with the term "American" continuing to be conflated with whiteness (Tuan 1998). These divisions remain even for those who are not immigrants, but second-, third-, and fourth-generation Asian-Americans. If even these native-born Americans are not seen as true Americans by native-born whites, how, then, are more recent immigrants from all backgrounds perceived? And how do these perceptions affect the immigrants' views of themselves?

Duany (1998) says, "Migrants bring their own cultural conceptions of their identity, which often do not coincide with the ideological constructions of the receiving societies" (147). This is one of the key concepts here; while an immigrant may very much want to identify as Colombian, or Vietnamese, or Trinidadian, the native-born Americans he or she encounters may simply place the immigrant individual into one of the previously conceived constructs in the United States. For most native-born Americans, this construct is at times racial—people are not seen as Jamaican, but black; not seen as Peruvian, but brown—and sometimes it is pan-ethnic—they're not seen as Cambodian, but Asian; not seen as Cuban, but Latino. At times, this outside identification can affect the individual's self-identification; at other times, the individual may challenge and resist this alter-identification.

> AUDREY (Brazilian): I thought that I was black in Brazil, but when you fill this application you always have to put your race in it? And I did once and I put black, Latino black, or something like that and they erased and put white people, so I don't know why they checked white. So, I don't really know.

Audrey's comments also show us that the definitions immigrants often bring with them is at odds with the classificatory system in the United States. She experienced native-born white Americans telling her that the way she perceived herself was not how she would be perceived in this new country. Audrey, and many of the other respondents, experienced "perceptual dissonance," the difference between how one views oneself versus how others view one (Rodriguez 2000).

Andy, a dark-skinned Cuban man, said he was often confused with

Afro-Americans. He said he was bothered by this at times; when he told people he was Cuban, they seem surprised that there were "black Cubans." Andy's experience was very different from Aaron's, a light-skinned Cuban, who said no one had ever confused his identity. Some of the other respondents also claimed that Americans, in general, could distinguish among different nationalities and were able to perceive when an individual was from Colombia versus Cuba versus Mexico, and so on. Those who believed that all native-born Americans knew their true identities also were usually the same individuals who did not see racism as an issue in the United States, nor felt they had experienced any discrimination.

There are both benefits and disadvantages for immigrants in being perceived as members of a pan-ethnic group. On the one hand, increased social, cultural, and even economic power acrues to one seen as a member of the far larger group, Latinos, rather than as a Venezuelan. However, at the same time, the refusal to see an individual as a member of any group other than a racial or pan-ethnic one is an expression of modern racism. Native-born white Americans often interpret this "optional ethnicity" (Waters 1990) to mean that anyone who feels strongly about their own ethnic or racial background does not want to be a true American. We saw this, for example, in the public outcry over immigrants' flying both Mexican and US flags at pro-immigration demonstrations in May 2006. For native-born Americans, it is unacceptable for people to come to the United States as immigrants and then hang on to their previous identities. According to most native-born Americans, one must choose to be an American in the United States, even while they simultaneously don't accept newcomers or their children as Americans.

Some immigrants recognized that they were grouped together with others in a pan-ethnic or racial categorization. In the same way that Ellen, from Trinidad, claimed that most white Americans saw all West Indians as the same, many of the Latino respondents thought that white and black Americans saw all Latinos as the same. As Laura said, "For them, all Latinos are from the same place." However, while grouping of all West Indians together clearly bothered Ellen, it did not bother Laura, nor apparently most of the other Latino respondents. Lisa, also from Colombia, said it did not bother her in any way that Americans called her Hispanic or Latino. Theresa, from Cambodia, did not seem to mind that she was categorized together with other Asian groups, either. Nor did the respondents in the focus group mind being seen as members of a pan-Asian group.

At times, respondents hinted that they understood they might not be identified as white by white Americans or as black by black Americans, placing them solidly in opposition to such binary classification. For example, when I asked a Mexican man about his race, he chose white. I then asked him if he thought a white person would classify him as white or black; he replied, "Black. *{What do you think a black person would classify you as?}* I think they'd say white." Or Ariel, from the Dominican Republic, who believed that white Americans could see that she was Hispanic and not black because "by our demeanor, the way we act, we act very differently from blacks." By placing herself in opposition to native-born blacks, Ariel believed her ethnicity was clear to all native-born Americans. Here we see very clearly the connection between the larger racial context and the self-identification of an immigrant.

Finally, those respondents who did not feel that Americans, white or black, could distinguish among the different nationalities often had the greatest problem with pan-ethnic categorizations. When I asked if native-born white or black Americans could tell the difference between groups, one man had this response:

> MANNY (Peruvian): No, I don't think so and I think that is where the problem begins, because we are all from different countries and they put us all in the same bag and they cannot identify if you are Peruvian, if you are Colombian, if you are Dominican. They don't even care and they just say you're Hispanic or they say you are Puerto Rican. *{And this is a problem?}* Yes, I believe so. *{Why?}* It's a problem because the culture that you develop and the culture that you were raised in your country has a lot to do with the type of person that you are. It marks you in reference to the capacity to work and how you want to project yourself towards your family. The feelings of your family, the emotions, the sentiments mark you a lot. We are all from Spanish-speaking countries but our formation in our countries is very different.

Manny also demonstrated his own biases: part of his problem with this categorization was that he believed that since Americans grouped him with all Hispanics, they often thought he was only capable of manual labor. Interestingly, in the same discussion, Manny said he was happy seeing Hispanics in high positions in this country, and that he was very proud and satisfied to see Hispanics succeeding. Karen, from Peru, also had a problem with being characterized with all other Hispanics, or even being mistaken for other Hispanic nationality groups. Karen, similarly to Manny, was not completely comfortable with this classification because of what she also perceived as the derogatory view of Hispanics. When I asked how she felt about this image, Karen responded:

> KAREN (Peruvian): I think it's just a submissive comment. It's something that I can't personally fight against. It's an image that has been around for a long period of time and still exists. We can't change the fact that they include all of us in the same bag. A lot of times Anglo-Saxons have developed a bad impression about Hispanics. . . . We supposedly don't respect other people's rights, a lot of times we break the law, we are dirty, we throw garbage in the street because of the culture we bring from our country. The Anglo-Saxon has seen this, they have observed it, and they have thrown everyone in the same bag.

Defining Others

The relationship between identity and race is further exemplified by the various ways the immigrant respondents spoke about other groups. The racialization of ethnic labels occurs "whereby terms that refer to specific ethnonational groups acquire racial meaning and form" (Kibria 2000:82). In the same way native-born white Americans tend to collapse various ethnic groups, such as Korean and Chinese, under the category "Asian," at various points my respondents did so as well. For example, Lee, a Jamaican man, would always say "Chinese" whenever he was referring to Asians in the United States. In Lee's case, he brought his experiences in Jamaica with him; in Jamaica, most of those from Asian countries were of Chinese ancestry. Karen, from Peru, made a similar claim when she said she believed there were simply three races, "white, black, and Chinese." Judith Goode and Jo Anne Schneider also make this point: "Such folk categories as 'Spanish' for all Latinos or 'Chinese' for all Asians are often used in everyday discourse by all groups, whether newcomer or established" (1994:69). Some of this Other-identification comes from the contact, or lack thereof, that immigrants have with other groups here in the United States.

Connections and Contacts. While most native-born Americans claim that racism and discrimination are a thing of the past, we still live in a society characterized by high levels of segregation (Massey and Denton 1993). And while overt racist tendencies on the part of whites have largely disappeared and most white Americans claim to support racial equality, as discussed earlier, high levels of residential segregation still exist in most US cities. This lack of interracial contact "exposes whites and blacks to very different socioeconomic environments" (1993:128); it also affects the residential location of most immigrants. So, in much the same way that the majority of native-born white Americans allege that they support racial integration and yet do not live this reality, the immigrants in my study also supported the ideas of integration and yet did not live in integrated environments. Additionally, more prominent than the interactions the immigrants had or did not have was the high level of connection the majority felt toward native-born white Americans, regardless of whether they had significant contact with these Americans.

The racial ideology that newcomers to this country learn (and that affects their identities) can and does have a great deal to do with whom they come into contact. Media images continue to project most Americans as white and often express derogatory images of racial minorities. If immigrants have limited contact with native-born Americans, their views will tend to reflect the stereotypes and ideas they receive from other sources, as we saw evidence of in the previous chapter. While we cannot hold onto the misguided belief that simply having increased contact between different groups leads to lower levels of prejudice, this limited contact also appears to lead them to believe that they have more in common with native-born white Americans than with native-born black Americans. The issues of contact and belief in shared commonalities are what I turn to in the next section.

Friendships. The majority of the immigrants I interviewed claimed that their friends were largely comprised of those from their pan-ethnic group; for instance, Colombians had friends from Peru, Uruguay, and Chile. This was true for several of the middle-class immigrants I spoke with, such as Freddy and Ginny, both from Peru, who, although they worked with many native-born Americans, said they found themselves connecting more with other Latinos. Additionally, several of the Latino immigrants commented on friendships with Puerto Ricans as well. Friendships with Puerto Ricans existed because of Puerto Ricans' status as part of the pan-ethnic category "Latino," regardless of their US citizenship status. The majority of immigrants accounted for this relationship with other Latinos as a function of a shared language, claiming this language barrier blocked friendships with those from other groups. This was true for some of the European immigrants I had discussions with as well; both a French immigrant and an Italian immigrant explained that although they spoke English well, they still felt most comfortable with people with whom they could speak their native language.

Andy, from Cuba, said all his friends were Hispanic, as did Laura, from Colombia. Some, however (such as Jesse, from Mexico, and Lisa, from Colombia) said that the majority of their friends were from their same nationality group. Some immigrants also found themselves placed alongside a group with whom, in their home countries, they might have had limited contact or, worse, negative perceptions. For example, at one of the literacy centers, I witnessed Russian and Ukrainian immigrants work together in class and discuss their friendships with one another. However, as their tutor pointed out to me, these students' nationality groups also had had a great deal of tension because of a long history of antagonism in their home countries.

While one can understand new relationships springing from language connections among those who have limited English proficiency, we also see such relationships within same-nationality groups—among those immigrants for whom language is *not* an issue. This was true for the Jamaican respondents, all of whom said that the majority of their friends were from Jamaica. Some exceptions, however, could be seen to this predominance of friendships among those in the same pan-ethnic or nationality group. One was Ellen, from Trinidad, who said she and her husband "moved to be near more black people." Nevertheless, this was the same couple who claimed that black people were lazy and unmotivated, and that they (she and her husband) preferred to associate with other West Indians. Language was an additional problem for Theresa, from Cambodia, who said she had very few friends outside of her family because of her inability to speak any language besides the Cambodian language that she spoke. Obviously, the pan-ethnic category "Asian" does not encompass solely one language.

Connections. The tendency of the respondents to maintain friendships with those from their same nationalities or pan-ethnic groups is consistent with the experiences of immigrants in the past—essentially, locating oneself among those from the same home country—and is an important factor to examine vis-à-vis the limited contact immigrants have with those from various backgrounds. Interestingly, when the respondent immigrants were asked whom they most felt connected to or identified with, the responses were very telling. Above all, the majority of the immigrants from Latin American countries claimed they felt most connected to Americans—white Americans. In answer to the question,

"Who do you feel the strongest connection to?" I received the following responses:

AUDREY: The white people, definitely.
LAURA (Colombian): The whites, I think.
LISA (Colombian): Americans. *{Whites? Blacks?}* Whites.
JESSE (Mexican): I also have American friends. *{White Americans?*
    Black Americans?} Whites, of course, whites.
MANNY (Peruvian): With the white people.

Those from the West Indian countries either said they felt strong connections only to others in their pan-ethnic category, or to black Americans. This type of connection was the case with Ellen and Doug, although, as we saw above, they continuously pointed out the distinctions between their own ethnic group and black Americans. Interestingly, while Ellen claimed that West Indians and Hispanics did not get along (and she correctly noted that they maintain very distinct neighborhoods within the city), Lee, another West Indian, mentioned that he did "hang with" Puerto Ricans as well as with other Jamaicans.

The Russian and Ukrainian immigrants were often living on social security assistance from the government, which meant they were at poverty level and, hence, at similar socioeconomic levels as many native-born racial minorities. Nonetheless, they believed there were few similarities between themselves and the latter groups. One explanation for the lack of association they felt could simply be skin color. Another, however, could be the fact that these immigrants were relatively well off in comparison to their previous lives, and so, as they articulated, they simply saw these other groups as lazy and unmotivated. Furthermore, by not necessarily perceiving themselves as poor and simultaneously viewing native-born white Americans as high in social status, these European immigrants believed there was greater common ground between themselves and native-born white Americans.

Intermarriage. I also asked these immigrants questions about intermarriage, both within their families and for their children. In particular, I asked how they would feel were their children to marry not only outside their ethnic groups, but outside their racial groups. While some respondents discussed intermarriages that had occurred within their families, and often said various members of their families took issue with the intermarriages, all insisted they did not have any problems with intermarriages of any kind. Furthermore, not one respondent claimed he or she would have any problem with their child marrying outside the ethnic or racial group. These responses are consistent with modern racism—subscribing to the principles of equality and being blind to race. However, when we consider some of the previous discussions, which were also consistent with modern racism—such as blaming racial minorities for any lower socioeconomic status they might have—we unfortunately must question whether this acceptance of intermarriage would really occur.

Alliances. Some immigrants who seemed to recognize that they shared similar experiences with native-born racial minorities, particularly in terms of racism and discrimination, were those who were more likely to be identified with native-born black Americans by the dominant group. For example, we saw numerous examples of Ellen, from Trinidad, speaking in derogatory terms about black Americans and not necessarily placing herself alongside this group in terms of her racial identity. However, she was the only immigrant I encountered who had begun her own nonprofit, neighborhood, grassroots organization, which included native-born black Americans and West Indians. Because Ellen lived in a part of the city that was predominantly black American and West Indian, establishing this organization made it unlikely that she would be successful if she only encouraged the participation of West Indians. However, there were few other West Indians working with black Americans in her local organization. It is possible that where Ellen saw power in numbers, others saw competition for scarce resources (Waters 1999).

Other immigrants working to improve social or economic conditions through local organizations focused on either a nationality group or on immigrants in general. For example, I worked with one organization that tried to keep immigrants from losing health-care benefits. Although this organization provided the opportunity for immigrant groups' representatives to discuss a variety of issues, it did not advance very much; it disbanded a short time after its creation, due to a lack of sufficient response. Interestingly, in asking respondents whether they thought there was a need for or benefit from these types of groups and/or alliances, they all believed that both immigrant groups and neighborhood organizations could be beneficial, although none (with the exception of Ellen) claimed to be involved in any such organization.

Conclusion

Although many of the interviewed immigrants, as we saw in the last chapter, acquired the current racial ideology that expresses a modern type of racism, they did not necessarily accept the current forms of racial categorization. They appeared to recognize a possibility that lay people and scholars overlook: that individuals may consider themselves different things at different times and in different contexts and may adopt different racial identities, depending on the contexts. One of the few scholars to recognize this variability in identification is Clara Rodriguez, who points out that there is no true and knowable self; that one's identity is relative and constantly negotiated through relationships and contexts (2000:xi). My research supports her contention; the majority of my respondents made a strong case for the variability of both race and ethnicity.

The various connections many of the immigrants felt toward others in their same pan-ethnic category, or only toward those in their nationality group, make sense when we think about our previous discussions of US ideologies. Immigrants come to the United States with the intention of making a better life for themselves. For them, this hope often means working more than one low-paying job, taking English classes whenever possible, and attempting to ensure a better life for their children. The limited contact they have with native-born racial minorities provides them with stereotypical beliefs that fuel their new racial ideology. In turn, this ideology means separating oneself from these other groups, and insisting that one not be placed in the same category.

We saw in the previous chapter that most of the immigrants, regardless of their ethnic background, participated in the type of modern racism expressed by native-born whites. However, in this chapter we saw that they did not necessarily fully accept all of the current racial ideologies. A key aspect to the dominant ideology is that individuals can be easily placed into one specific racial category; in particular, this dominant racial ideology rests on a binary racial analysis. The immigrants in my study challenged this assumption; they traversed the spectrum of racial categories, at times completely rejecting racial categorization and, at other times, choosing an identification based on a combination of racial and ethnic markers. Nevertheless, similarly to immigrants in the past, among the immigrants in my study there continued to be a strong and consistent separation from African-Americans.

Previous groups of immigrants (i.e., Southern and Eastern

Europeans) eventually became white and American. In the end, they were able to conceive of themselves as having fulfilled the American Dream. Immigrants now want the same dream, but they are not likely to become part of this larger group of white ethnics. They also do not conceive of themselves as ever becoming truly American. Does this mean they will be denied this dream? And, if so, will they begin to see more connections and similarities between themselves and native-born racial minorities, who historically have been denied the dream by dominant whites? Or will they continue to see benefits in separating and distancing themselves from native-born black Americans? In choosing this latter option, they are helping to reproduce the very system into which they have entered; one that places black Americans perpetually on the bottom of the social status scale.

7

Racial Reproduction Revisited

I BEGAN THIS STUDY WITH THE hope of exploring how racial ideology is passed on to new members of society and how this ideology affects the development of their identities. What I discovered was that this racial knowledge acquisition, racial knowledge expression, and identity development lead to racial reproduction. Immigrants develop a racial habitus, which, in turn, helps to assure the continuation of the dominant ideology.

Recently, various scholars have explored the idea that we are entering a racialized world divided along black-nonblack lines, rather than the more commonly held beliefs of a black-white dichotomy (Gans 1999, Lee et al. 2003, Yancey 2003, 2006). As George Yancey explains, the majority of newer immigrant groups are following in the paths of previous immigrant groups; they are assimilating into a white racial status and helping to further alienate black Americans from the rest of US society (2003). Eduardo Bonilla-Silva and Karen Glover maintain that we are seeing the emergence of a tri-racial system, with whites in one category, honorary whites (such as Japanese Americans and Middle Eastern Americans) in a second category, and "collective blacks" in a third category (2004:151).

My research for this book indicates that while the new immigrant groups I interviewed certainly aimed to distance themselves from native-born black Americans, they were not, however, striving for a white racial identity. As we witnessed, they were subscribing to much of the same racial rhetoric and ideology—modern racism—that native-born white Americans have, but they were simultaneously creating new and separate racial identities. These identities were often at odds with the current racial schemes put forth by political, academic, and lay per-

137

sons. Few of these new immigrants were comfortable with the narrow, strict racial choices offered them. One of the most important things this teaches us, then, is that perhaps we need to alter our understanding of racial identity to better reflect multiracial and ethnic identities while simultaneously recognizing that modern racism is being reproduced by new immigrants. This chapter will highlight the major contributions of my research and explore this "new racial divide" and what it means for the future of race and racism in this country.

Research Findings: Racial Reproduction

All individuals living in the United States are exposed to a certain racial social structure, specific to this country. This structure encompasses all of our major institutions and organizations, each of which helps to create and promote the dominant racial ideology. Currently, the dominant racial ideology in the United States is modern racism, a belief that opportunity and success are available to anyone who wants them and works hard, that overt and blatant forms of racism are not only unacceptable but have been largely rejected and illegalized, and that we live now in a society where no one is judged by the color of their skin. Through the agents of these institutions and organizations, the culture, and the existing racial configuration (i.e., neighborhood segregation), immigrants come to learn this dominant racial ideology. After absorbing this, they then readjust their habitus to reflect their new knowledge, which in turn affects the development of their own racial identities. The circle is complete: the immigrant has now become part of the larger racial social structure in helping to promote the dominant ideologies, and the entire process is reproduced.

Knowledge of the US Racial Hierarchy

The first stage of learning racial knowledge actually occurs while the immigrant is still in his or her home country. Individuals are initially socialized according to their nation's classification scheme; concurrently, the individual contemplating immigration begins to learn about race in the United States from media sources and from friends and family who previously immigrated to the United States. Once immigrants arrive here, they are promptly exposed to the current racial ideology and the corresponding racial hierarchy. In essence, new immigrants, just like those before them, learn to value whiteness and devalue blackness. A predominant source of this exposure for immigrants is immigrant-service organizations. Further, in order for the process of reproduction to occur, agents of these organizations must help to teach the current ideology.

My research shows that often these agents are not aware of their role in the reproduction process. Regardless of intent, by either ignoring the role race plays in individuals' lives or denying that they "see race," the majority of socialization agents are chief reproducers of modern racism. Consistent with the modern racism evident among most native-born white Americans, these agents help to uphold the current racial ideology through their language, beliefs, actions, and cultural resources. Specifically, they promote the idea that anyone who works hard enough can make it in the United States, that there are no barriers to this success, and that we all live in a color-blind society. Along with the idea of meritocracy comes the notion that those who are not successful are simply not working hard enough and only have themselves to blame for their predicament. In blaming the victims, these agents establish a precedent for immigrants to have only themselves to blame for any potential lack of achievement: the message is, if racism and discrimination do not exist, then there are no barriers to immigrants' success. As a corollary: if these factors do not impinge on immigrants' accomplishments, then certainly many native-born black Americans, who have been here longer and are citizens of this country, have no excuse for their low socioeconomic status in this society.

Our system of racial hierarchy means that those in positions of power tend, predominantly, to be white Americans; this reality is reflected in the immigrant-service organizations I studied. Immigrants see clearly that those in power and control are principally native-born white Americans. None of the services' agents, however, pointed to historical racism and discrimination as the explanation for this; instead, they provided knowledge affirming that the United States was a meritocracy. These "American representatives"—those who embody an American in the eyes of the recent immigrants—not only helped to promote and reproduce dominant racial ideologies, but their very presence as members of the dominant race in positions of power and authority upheld the value placed on whiteness.

Reflective of the racial segregation evident in society at large, the lower-class immigrants spent a majority of their time, whether it was at work or in the community, with others from their same pan-ethnic or specific nationality group. For many immigrants, the only native-born Americans they encountered were those from whom they learned English or received practical advice and resources. Recent middle-class immigrants spent their time either with other immigrants of similar cultural and social backgrounds, or with native-born white Americans. Therefore, for all immigrants, the underlying social context provided by the agents of socialization was further evidence that to become an American, one must accept particular American values. Hence, immigrants came to believe that only those who accepted the right cultural values would succeed in the United States. A major part of these cultural values is the ideology of modern racism. Immigrants come here in search of the American Dream; in search of a better life for themselves and, often, for their children. This dream entails a strong belief in hard work, individualism, and meritocracy, and, consistent with the dominant racial ideology, contradicts the belief that racism exists in the United States.

Expression of Racial Knowledge

Newer immigrants' increasing awareness of the US racial structure and hierarchy, the representatives teaching them both American Dream and racial ideologies, and the cultural resources to which they are exposed all create what I term a "racial habitus." In turn, this racial habitus provides the immigrant with the knowledge of racial ideology expressions we see in native-born white Americans.

It became clear very quickly from speaking with the interviewed immigrants, both working-class and professional, that their racial ideology expressions were consistent with the modern racism currently existing in the United States (Bobo, Kluegel, and Smith 1997, Gallagher 2003, Hughes 1998). Firmly believing that everyone in the United States should be, and was, treated equally, they therefore believed that people who did not succeed had only themselves to blame. In particular, when discussing racial minorities—especially black Americans—the majority of immigrants I spoke with maintained that any lack of success or increased status for such groups was due, respectively, to a lack of motivation or a positive work ethic. Immigrants all come here searching for and believing in the American Dream; based on my research, the only way for them to preserve that dream is to believe that those who do not succeed have created their own destinies.

While the majority of the immigrants in this study denied the existence of racism, they themselves showed expressions of it, not just in their assumptions about native-born black Americans, but also in the very language that they used to describe who an American actually was. They consistently used the term "American" for the unmarked category of "white Americans" and the qualifier "black" anytime they were referring to native-born black Americans. To the immigrants, a real American was a white American, and no one else could quite achieve the same status.

Most of the immigrants I spoke with had experienced some form of discrimination; however, rather than conceiving of the discrimination as racism, the majority perceived these experiences as simple "miscommunications" because of language barriers. Even those who believed they had experienced racial discrimination, such as some of the West Indian respondents, still maintained that this discrimination was not a barrier to success.

By believing that native-born white Americans were the only real Americans, and by adopting the same racial ideology of modern racism expressed by these native-born Americans, these immigrants were constructing their own racial habitus. This habitus in turn led them to become even more American than they realized.

Racial Knowledge Affects Immigrants' Racial Identity

Immigrant identity development is most definitively affected by their racial habitus. Nonetheless, a national identity and a racial or ethnic one are not necessarily the same things. My study provides support for the idea that immigrants acquire and then express current racial ideologies; I also found that they do not necessarily accept the idea that they, too, can become Americans. Consistent with their belief that true Americans are white Americans, the majority believes that they will never become "full" Americans or even, in some cases, "hyphenated" Americans. Some respondents could not accept the idea that they would *ever* be American, with or without hyphenation, regardless of their length of time spent in the United States. Others felt that a "hyphenation identification" would develop only after they had become citizens. However, all of the respondents recognized that their children would take on this hyphenated identity, being partly of this new world and partly of the old. A clear reason for this denial of an American identity stemmed from the continued belief that only whites were true Americans. We repeatedly witnessed immigrants express this viewpoint in the language they chose; for example, using the word "American" to denote a white status and giving all others a qualifier (as in "black Americans").

Nevertheless, within the context of locating a new identity in this host country, these immigrants expressed some limited challenges to the racial system. Race is a system of power; for the dominant racial group, part of that power comes from attaching racial category designations to others (Kibria 1998). The immigrants appeared to challenge these externally imposed classifications. Many refused to accept the strict white-black binary constructions of race, retaining a nationality or ethnic identity separate and unrelated to race. It is possible that the rejection of strict racial categories can eventually lead to a challenge of racial categories altogether.

European immigrants to the United States in the twentieth century eventually became white ethnics, as well as primarily unhyphenated Americans. New immigrants and their children are denied this option by the dominant racial group and often by their own designations. The majority of immigrants currently arriving in the United States are not perceived as white by the dominant, or subordinate, population. Does this mean they will also be denied attainment of the American Dream? The immigrants in my study accepted the white mainstream ethic; it remains to be seen, however, if the more they encounter discrimination, the more they will perceive it as racial discrimination and become disabused of this ethic.

If, on the other hand, newcomers continue to respond to discrimination by viewing it as something temporary and by attributing it to their foreigner status, as the immigrants in my study did, then they will continue to compare themselves to white Americans (Ogbu 1990a). Desire for association with white Americans means not finding any similarities or commonalities with native-born black Americans, whether those be racial or cultural connections.

Immigrants aspiring to the American Dream are not immune to the reality that those living that dream tend to be white. Contrasting this, new immigrants are clearly able to recognize the demographics of the poor in this country; but they believe lack of hard work on the part of those in lower socioeconomic strata is the source of those groups' status. By buying into the American Dream, in essence, immigrants are buying into white racism and the white racial system. Striving for middle-class status is not only about class, but is also a recognition on the part of immigrants of which groups are in the upper and lower classes. Denial of the existence of racism and insistence on a color-blind viewpoint—viewing all people the same, regardless of race—are components of the process of racial reproduction. Modern racism is being reproduced among new members of society and, therefore, is reproduced in society as a whole.

What Happens Now?

My intent in studying recent immigrants was to understand the process of racial knowledge acquisition in its early stages. However, it is possible that the longer a nonwhite immigrant lives in the United States, the more likely he or she is to experience racial discrimination. It is also possible that continued experiences of racism might lead the immigrant to be less supportive of the American Dream ideology, a component of modern racism, and more likely to acknowledge and recognize the limitations to this dream—limitations native-born black Americans have always experienced. Perhaps after having lived in the United States for ten or twenty years, immigrants will be less able to justify the discrimination they experience and more willing to make alliances with other racial minority groups. On the other hand, perhaps we will find immigrants retaining belief in the American Dream, either because they had achieved success or because they still believed they would, and, therefore, holding onto the ideologies they received from the dominant racial group.

What is more, there is a self-selection process in immigration. All the immigrants I interviewed had moved here to achieve a better life for themselves and (for some) their children. This self-selection process could also lead to a refusal to acknowledge obstacles, such as racism, that might impair success. Therefore, as some research on the second generation has begun to do, it is increasingly important to look at the race socialization process for the children of immigrants—those who did not have a choice about immigrating. How does their racial knowledge acquisition process differ from their parents' process? How do they express this knowledge? And, in turn, how does the racial ideology affect their own identities? Are their identities different from those that their parents expected they would develop?

Theoretical Implications

This research has theoretical importance by adding to the general literature on structural racism, racial formation, whiteness studies, immigrant racial identity theory, and, most especially, social reproduction theory. While numerous authors have examined the class implications of social reproduction theory, few authors have specifically explored the ways in which race, racial inequality, and racism are socially reproduced. Thus, by linking racial identity to the larger racial social structure, I was able to examine race reproduction—the process of reproducing racism and racial inequality.

What I discovered from my research on immigrants is that the racial reproduction process, similar in many ways to the class reproduction process, is a multidimensional and ongoing process. Individuals learn racial knowledge and racial ideology from a variety of resources. In particular, just as class reproduction occurs predominantly through family and school socialization, the areas of greatest social impact for children, racial reproduction also occurs primarily through these socializing agents. Immigrants receive an education from the services they use; part of this education is about race. We see the expressions of this racial awareness through the racial habitus an immigrant develops. This habitus, in turn, affects the identity construction of the immigrant, leading to an identity at least partly based on this racial awareness. Finally, the immigrant then becomes part of the very system he or she is learning, helping to reproduce the system itself. This process repeats itself for all members of society. This process is racial reproduction.

Another area of theoretical importance is racialization processes. Previous research on racialization (Omi and Winant 1994, Espiritu 1992, Bashi 1998) has consistently examined this process for groups as a whole, whereas my research examines this process for the individual. What we have seen is that immigrants undergoing the racialization process do not fully accept the classifications they are placed in by the dominant racial majority group, raising the possibility of challenges to the racial system. The more recent works exploring alternatives to the dominant black-white racial identity paradigm are most useful in this area (Lee et al. 2003, Yancey 2003, Gans 1999). However, contrary to what many of these authors claim is a new black-nonblack divide, my study points to a more fluid color line, with immigrants retaining their belief that they are separate from both whites and blacks alike. Perhaps by recognizing that most new immigrants, adopting more flexible and multiracial identities, are challenging and altering the racial identity lines in the United States, we should welcome these challenges to racial and ethnic boundaries. Yet we must recognize the fact that these new immigrants are following in the footsteps of their immigrant predecessors—not in wanting to achieve a white racial identity, but in believing that native-born black Americans are on the lower end of the racial hierarchy due to their own failures and lack of hard work. This adoption of modern racism means that the new immigrants are helping to re-create the very system they are learning. In doing so, they are helping to ensure native-born black Americans remain on the bottom of this hierarchy.

Societal Implications

It is possible from this study for policy makers and community leaders to develop programs that target immigrant groups—both immigrant children and adults—and their knowledge of racial relations in the

United States. We have learned from educating white students that awareness of the development of racism increases students' interest and participation in social change (Tatum 1994). Educating immigrants on the history of US racial relations—including slavery, colonization, and genocide—as well as on the causes and consequences of minority poverty might decrease immigrants' desire to distance themselves from native-born black Americans and increase their potential to join multiracial coalitions. If cultural agents, rather than ignoring race and racism in the resources they provide immigrants, instead emphasized these topics, it is possible that new immigrants would develop a different understanding of race relations and racism in the United States. Scholars have spent a considerable amount of time, particularly since the Los Angeles riots of 1992, examining interracial tensions (Ikemoto 2000, Sanchez 1997, Goode and Schneider 1994, Miles 1992). In particular, increased attention has been given to the strains between the communities of native-born black Americans and immigrants (Weitzer 1987, Jo 1992, Cheng and Espiritu 1989). Although my study shows evidence that new immigrants accept the dominant racial ideologies, it is still possible that these tensions could be reduced by decreased acceptance of the dominant racial category constructions. As we saw, the immigrants in my study largely rejected the categories the government (and native-born Americans) asked them to choose. Instead, they tended to adopt more multiracial, or strictly national, identities. In doing so, they were challenging the existing racial hierarchy in one way. By both learning about, and then possibly experiencing, barriers to success, all minorities, regardless of racial affiliation, might find common cause with each other.

We can use what occurs for immigrants in the process of acquiring racial knowledge to sensitize us to how race reproduction occurs for native-born Americans as well. It is critical for those who are, or want to be, involved in dismantling racism to identify the mechanisms and processes by which new members of society are introduced to white racism and the value of white identity. In order to build a nonracist society, we must encourage multiracial coalitions and movements that disrupt the development of white racism and white racial identity.

Appendix A:
Notes on Research and Methods

Overview of Research

I began my research by volunteering at a local literacy center, Literacy Volunteers of Eastern City (LVEC), which offers both literacy and English as a Second Language (ESL) classes. This nonprofit organization is comprised of one main center (housing the administrative staff and the majority of the classes) and approximately five satellite centers located throughout the city, where classes are held one to three times a week. The main office conducts classes on a daily basis; it offers literacy and ESL courses in the mornings and evenings on alternate days, as well as citizenship lessons several times a week and computer classes. It also provides various other resources for students, such as computers, reading materials, and job information. Classes run on twelve-week sessions with a four-week summer session. The centers cater to approximately 350 students at any one time, from a variety of ethnic backgrounds. There are frequently drives to recruit new volunteer tutors, with orientation classes for these teachers once every six months. As the organization is nonprofit, the tutors are overseen by a board of directors consisting of nineteen members and only nine paid staff, several of whom work part time.

After volunteering for six months at the centers, I began looking for potential respondents to interview. I attempted to gain a sample reflective of the larger surrounding immigrant population (see Chapter 2), a relatively equal number of men and women, and those who had immigrated to the United States in the previous ten to fifteen years. I placed signs, which included my contact information, at the main office, stating that I was conducting a research study on immigrant experience, and would pay respondents fifteen dollars for their time. Additionally, after recognizing that there would be a significant number of Spanish-speaking adults I wanted to interview, I hired a research assistant to conduct interviews in Spanish.

I conducted a total of thirty-four interviews. Of the interviewed immigrants, sixteen were from Latin America, five from the West Indies, two from Asia, and four from Europe. The majority of these immigrants had immigrated in the past five to ten years. I also conducted one focus group comprised of four adults from three Asian countries (Vietnam, China, Cambodia). I conducted formal interviews with eight individuals working with immigrants; within one center, I spoke to two upper-level administrators, two assistant staff members, and two tutors. Additionally, at a second center providing services to immigrants, I spoke to two staff members (see Appendix B).

While these interviews are at the core of my research, what is important to recognize is that this study focuses on the process and mechanisms involved in learning racial knowledge and forming a racial identity in relation to this knowledge. Because I believe that race and racial identity are social constructions, I also believe they change over time and in different contexts. Therefore, I do not conceive of my study as the final interpretation of the phenomenon of racial reproduction and, instead, maintain that this process is constantly evolving and that I have studied only some aspects of it.

Throughout the year and a half I was involved in my research, I participated in a grassroots organization comprised of various members of the community working to retain health-care benefits for immigrants. This group included leaders of various immigrant communities (e.g., West Indian, Vietnamese, Cambodian) and activist leaders from the general community. Finally, my research was also informed by my participation first as a member and later as an officer in another grassroots organization, led by a West Indian immigrant whose goal was to improve the community environment.

Methodological Issues: Sources of Errors

Reactions to Researcher and Research

While it has long been argued in sociology that the race of the interviewer may affect the respondents in research (Rhodes 1994), it was during the politically charged climate of the 1960s that the practice of "racial matching" came into effect. Essentially, this argument holds that researchers should be of the same racial background as their subjects. The reasoning for this matching is several-fold: first, that white researchers were incapable of grasping the realities of black life. Second, that because of their differing life experiences, blacks and whites approach the subject of race very differently. Third, and most important, black scholars at that time argued that the general mistrust toward all white researchers would prohibit these researchers from conducting research in black communities (Winddance Twine and Warren 2000).

Despite some early critics of this methodological approach (Merton 1972), only fairly recently have researchers begun to challenge the idea of racial matching, recognizing that, in fact, there can be benefits and disadvantages to both insider and outsider status (Gallagher 2000, Beoku-Betts 1994). As some of these researchers acknowledge, simply having insider status with regard to race does not preclude other social characteristics from potentially affecting the research. Further, such insider status may be more an assumption than a reality, with the insider status still needing to be negotiated. Finally, other researchers have recognized that insider status can present barriers in that researchers with such status are often expected to conform to the cultural norms of the community, such as traditional gender norms (Hondagneu-Sotelo 1994).

In terms of outsider status, as some researchers argue, cross-ethnic research involving racial or ethnic differences between the researcher and the subjects can actually be successful in that interviewees often strive to explain their ethnic experiences to those who do not share them (Rubin and Rubin 1995). Essentially, qualitative/ethnographic researchers now seem to agree that, since there can be benefits and disadvantages to both insider and outsider status, "it is optimal to have both racial insiders and outsiders conducting research because they reveal different—not better—kinds of knowledge (Winddance Twine and Warren 2000:13).

As an outsider—a native-born, white American woman—I was aware of these various issues. It was with this awareness in mind that I chose to hire an assistant to conduct a number of the interviews. While clearly I could not accomplish this insider/outsider status in relation to all of my respondents (e.g., I could not hire the numerous assistants I would have needed for all of the various Asian cultures and languages represented in the interviews), I attempted to address some of the outsider-status issues in terms of language and ethnicity. Keeping in mind the percentage of Spanish-speaking immigrants in the Northeast area where my study was located, I enlisted the aid of a Puerto Rican woman to conduct interviews in Spanish. Margie was one of the assistant staff members at the center where I conducted my observations; and after I told her about my research, she offered to help in any way she could. Following several unsuccessful attempts to find relatively recent immigrants from Latin America with enough English language skills for me to conduct a successful interview, I approached Margie to see if she would be interested in having me hire her to conduct some interviews. After she agreed, we met twice to go over the research in more detail and the interview guide in depth. I explained the research questions and the intricacies of interviewing, and we thoroughly discussed the research guide. Margie then accompanied me on an interview and observed the interview method. After she conducted two of her own interviews and had translated and transcribed them, we met again to go over her interviews in detail. In that way, I was able to point out various matters, such as the areas where she needed to probe more or to lead less. After she had conducted two more interviews, we again met and went through the interviews in the same way. I became fully confident in Margie's abilities as an interviewer and that she understood the objective of the interviewing process.

Margie's insider status as a Latina may well have opened the door to immigrants who might have been unwilling to speak to me and clearly provided the opportunity to interview a significant number of immigrants who did not speak English well enough for an English-language interview. She also had insider status because many immigrants she interviewed were familiar with her and considered her a member of the community. I gave her the go-ahead to interview those immigrants she knew outside of LVEC, so as not to limit her to only those she came in contact with at the center. Having Margie was an advantage for another reason as well: since she is not an immigrant, those she interviewed were forced to explain in greater detail experiences they felt she could not relate to. Additionally, as both Margie and several of the respondents in her interviews pointed out, being a Puerto Rican Latino/a is not the same as being an immigrant Latino/a from Latin America.

One issue I tried to be aware of continually when interviewing immigrants was that "for a researcher working in immigrant communities, questions about race can be particularly tricky" (Islam 2000:41). While it is generally agreed that categories of race are neither static nor stable (Omi and Winant 1994), it is especially difficult to ask questions about race when dealing with transnational concepts. Essentially, what race means in the United States and what it means in the Dominican

Republic, for example, can be very different. What must occur, then, is a constant problematizing of race: using every possible means to examine the immigrant concept of race and not making assumptions about the meaning of race, or racism, based on the researchers' understandings of the concept (Islam 2000). By asking questions throughout the interview about the respondents' racial perceptions of others, my objective was to examine the simultaneous processes of racial categorization and racial identity development. I believe this format for questioning enabled me to examine the ways in which immigrant racial ideology affects racial perceptions and racial identity. Investigating the way immigrants talk about race and racism, how they explore the dimensions of their racial and ethnic identities, and how these concepts are related to each other helps us understand the process of racial reproduction.

Appendix B: Interviewees

Immigrant Respondents

Name	Age	Nationality	Migration Year
1. Lisa R.	Late 20s	Colombian	1999
2. Laura M.	Late 20s	Colombian	1999
3. Craig M.	Mid-30s	Colombian	1999
4. Ariel R.	Early 30s	Dominican	1994
5. Ellen S.	Mid-40s	Trinidadian	1983
6. Doug S.	Late 40s	Trinidadian	1983
7. Paula C.	Early 40s	Jamaican	1994
8. Aaron H.	Early 70s	Cuban	1996
9. Karen P.	Early 30s	Peruvian	2000
10. Claire D.	Mid-30s	Jamaican	1992
11. Manny G.	Early 30s	Peruvian	2000
12. Audrey D.	Late 20s	Brazilian	1999
13. Theresa L.	Late 20s	Cambodian	1996
14. Lee W.	Mid-30s	Jamaican	1988
15. Jesse C.	Early 20s	Mexican	1994
16. Stacy L.	Mid-30s	Peruvian	2000
17. Freddy S.	Mid-50s	Peruvian	1970
18. Geraldo M.	Mid-40s	Colombian	1998
19. Pamela L.	Mid-40s	Spanish	1998
20. Ginny T.	Mid-30s	Peruvian	2004
21. Lori P.	Mid-30s	French	1999
22. Janet D.	Late 50s	Dominican	1991
23. Andy C.	Mid-30s	Cuban	1995
24. Patty S.	Mid-50s	English	1979
25. Hilda C.	Early 40s	Ecuadorian	1982
26. Franny Z.	Early 30s	Italian	1998
27. Natalie T.	Early 20s	Cambodian	1990

Staff/Tutors

Name	Role at Agency	Approximate Age	Race
1. Polly Q.	Tutor	Mid-40s	Native-born white American
2. Maggie A.	Staff	Late 20s	Puerto Rican
3. Greg D.	Staff	Mid-50s	Native-born white American
4. Bonnie O.	Staff	Early 30s	Native-born white American
5. Yolanda G.	Staff	Early 30s	Native-born black American
6. Diane S.	Director, religious program	Early 50s	Native-born white American
7. Dana L.	Staff, religious program	Mid-30s	Native-born white European
8. Martha H.	Director, nonprofit agency	Mid-50s	Native-born white American

Bibliography

Alba, Richard. 1985. *Italian Americans: Into the Twilight.* Englewood Cliffs, NJ: Prentice Hall.

———. 1990. *Ethnicity in America: The Transformation of White America.* New Haven, CT: Yale University Press.

Alba, Richard, and Victor Nee. 2003. *Remaking the American Mainstream: Assimilation and Contemporary Immigration.* Cambridge, MA: Harvard University Press.

Almageur, Tomas. 1994. *Racial Fault Lines: The Historical Origins of White Supremacy in California.* Berkeley: University of California Press.

Altimari, Daniela. 2002. "The Gray Russians." *Hartford Courant.* July 8: A1, A6.

Azuma, Eiichiro. 1994. "Interethnic Conflict under Racial Subordination: Japanese Immigrants and their Asian Neighbors in Walnut Grove, CA, 1908–1941." *Amerasia Journal* 20(2): 27–56.

Bailey, Benjamin. 2006. "Black and Latino: Dominican Americans Negotiate Racial Worlds," in *Mixed Messages: Multiracial Identities in the "Color-Blind" Era*, ed., David Brunsma, pp. 481–507. Boulder, CO: Lynne Rienner.

Barkan, Elliot. 2006. "Introduction: Immigration, Incorporation, Assimilation, and the Limits of Transnationalism." *Journal of American Ethnic History* 25(2/3): 33-47.

Barrett, James, and David Roediger. 1997. "In-Between Peoples: Race, Nationality, and the 'New Immigrant' Working Class." *Journal of American Ethnic History* (Spring): 3–44.

Bashi, Vilna. 1998. "Racial Categories Matter Because Racial Hierarchies Matter: A Commentary." *Ethnic and Racial Studies* 21(5): 959–968.

Beoku-Betts, Josephine. 1994. "When Black is Not Enough: Doing Field Research Among Gullah Women." *NWSA Journal* 6(3): 413–433.

Berger, Maurice. 1999. *White Lies: Race and the Myth of Whiteness.* New York: Ferrar, Straus, and Giroux.

Berrol, Selma Cantor. 1995. *Growing Up American.* New York: Twayne.

Blumer, Herbert. 1958. "Race Prejudice as a Sense of Group Position." *Pacific Sociological Review* 1(1):3–7.

Bobo, Lawrence. 1988. "Group Conflict, Prejudice, and the Paradox of Contemporary Racial Attitudes." In *Eliminating Racism: Profiles in Controversy.* Edited by Phyllis A. Katz and D. A. Taylor. New York: Plenum Press.

———. 2002. *Prismatic Metropolis: Inequality in Los Angeles.* New York: Russell Sage Foundation.

———. 2004. "Inequalities that Endure? Racial Ideology, Amercian Politics, and the Peculiar Role of the Social Sciences." Pp.13–42 in *The Changing Terrain of Race and Ethnicity.* Edited by Maria Krysan and Amanda E. Lewis. New York: Russell Sage Foundation.

Bobo, Lawrence, James R. Kluegel, and Ryan A. Smith. 1997. "Laissez-Faire Racism: The Crystallization of a Kinder, Gentler, Antiblack Ideology." Pp. 15–42 in *Racial Attitudes in the 1990's.* Edited by Steven A. Tuch and Jack K. Martin. Westport, CT: Draeger.

Bonilla-Silva, Eduardo. 1996. "Rethinking Racism: Toward a Structural Interpretation." *American Sociological Review* 62: 465–480.

———. 2001. *White Supremacy and Racism in the Post-Civil Rights Era.* Boulder, CO: Lynne Rienner.

———. 2003. *Racism Without Racists: Color-Blind Racism and the Persistence of Racial Inequality in the United States.* Lanham, MD: Rowman and Littlefield.

Bonilla-Silva, Eduardo, and Karen S. Glover. 2004. "We Are All Americans: The Latin Americanization of Race Relations in the United States." Pp.149–183 in *The Changing Terrain of Race and Ethnicity.* Edited by Maria Krysan and Amanda E. Lewis. New York: Russell Sage Foundation.

Bourdieu, Pierre. 1977. *Outline of a Theory of Practice.* Cambridge: Cambridge University Press.

———. 1984. *Distinction: A Social Critique of the Judgement of Taste.* London, England: Routledge and Kegan Paul.

———. 1990. *In Other Words: Essays Towards a Reflexive Sociology.* Stanford, CA: Stanford University Press.

———. 1992. *The Logic of Practice.* Stanford, CA: Stanford University Press.

Bourdieu, Pierre, and Loic J. D. Wacquant. 1992. *An Invitation to Reflexive Sociology.* Chicago: University of Chicago Press.

Bowles, Samuel, and Herbert Gintis. 1976. *Schooling in Capitalist America.* New York: Basic Books.

Brimelow, Peter. 1995. *Alien Nation: Common Sense About America's Immigration Disaster.* New York: Random House

Brodkin Sacks, Karen. 1998. *How Jews Became White Folks and What That Says About Race in America.* New Brunswick, NJ: Rutgers University Press.

Charmaz, Kathy. 1983. "The Grounded Theory Method: An Explication and Interpretation." Pp. 109–126 in *Contemporary Filed Research: A Collection of Readings.* Edited by Robert M. Emerson. Prospect Heights, IL: Waveland Press.

Cheng, Lucie, and Yen Le Espiritu. 1989. "Korean Businesses in Black and Hispanic Neighborhoods: A Study of Intergroup Relations." *Sociological Perspectives* 32(4): 521–534.

Cole, David. 1999. *No Equal Justice: Race and Class in the American Criminal Justice System.* New York: The New Press.

Collins, Sharon. 1997. *Black Corporate Executives: The Making and Breaking of a Black Middle Class.* Philadelphia: Temple University Press.

Cose, Ellis. 1993. *The Rage of a Privileged Class.* New York: Harper Collins.

Crompton, Rosemary. 2006. "Class and Family." *Sociological Review* 54(4): 658–677.

Cross, William E. 1985. "Black Identity: Discovering the Distinction Between Personal Identity and Reference Group Orientation." In *Beginnings: The Social and Affective Development of Black Children.* Edited by Margaret Beale Spencer, Geraldine Kearse Brookins, and Walter Recharde Allen. Hillsdale, NJ: L. Erlbaum.

———. 1991. *Shades of Black: Diversity in African American Identity.* Philadelphia: Temple University Press.

de la Fuente, Alejandro. 2001. "The Resurgence of Racism in Cuba." *NACLA: Report on the Americas* 34(6): 29–34.

Delgado, Richard, and Jean Stefancic, eds. 1997. *Critical White Studies: Looking Behind the Mirror.* Philadelphia: Temple University Press.

Dominguez, Virginia. 1978. "Show Your Colors: Ethnic Divisiveness Among Caribbean Migrants." *Migration Today* 6(1): 5–9.

D'Souza, Dinesh. 1995. *The End of Racism: Principles for a Multiracial Society.* New York: Free Press.

Duany, Jorge. 1998. "Reconstructing Racial Identity: Ethnicity, Color, and Class Among Dominicans in the U.S. and Puerto Rico." *Latin American Perspectives* 25(3): 147–172.

Espiritu, Yen Le. 1992. *Asian American Panethnicity: Bridging Institutions and Identities.* Philadelphia: Temple University Press.

Essed, Philomena. 1991. *Understanding Everyday Racism: An Interdisciplinary Theory.* Newbury Park, CA: Sage Publications.

Feagin, Joe. 2000. *Racist America: Roots, Current Realities, and Future Reparations.* New York: Routledge.

Feagin, Joe, and Hernan Vera. 1995. *White Racism: The Basics.* New York: Routledge.

Feagin, Joe, and Melvin Sikes. 1994. *Living with Racism: The Black Middle Class Experience.* Boston: Beacon Press.

Fernandez, Ronald. 2000. *America's Banquet of Cultures: Harnessing Ethnicity, Race, and Immigration in the Twenty-First Century.* Westport, CT: Praeger.

———. 2001. "Our Civilized Neighbors: Greater Hartford's West Indians." *Hartford Courant.* January 5: A11.

Foner, Nancy. 1985. "Race and Color: Jamaican Migrants in London and New York City." *International Migration Review* 19(4): 708–727.

———. 1998. "West Indian Identity in the Diaspora: Comparative and Historical Perspectives." *Latin American Perspective* 25(3): 173–188.

Foner, Nancy, ed. 2001. *New Immigrants in New York*. New York: Columbia University Press.

Foreman, Tyrone A. 2004. "Color-Blind Racism and Racial Indifference: The Role of Racial Apathy in Facilitating Enduring Inequalities." Pp. 43–66 in *The Changing Terrain of Race and Ethnicity*. Edited by Maria Krysan and Amanda E. Lewis. New York: Russell Sage Foundation.

Fox, Geoffrey. 1996. *Hispanic Nation: Culture, Politics, and the Construction of Identity*. Tucson: University of Arizona Press.

Frankenberg, Ruth. 1993. *White Women, Race Matters: The Social Construction of Whiteness*. Minneapolis: University of Minnesota Press.

Gallagher, Charles. 2000. "White Like Me? Methods, Meaning, and Manipulation in the Field of White Studies." Pp. 67–92 in *Racing Research, Researching Race*. Edited by France Winddance Twine and Jonathan W. Warren. New York: New York University Press.

———. "Color-Blind Privilege: The Social and Political Functions of Erasing the Color Line in Post-Race America." *Race, Gender, and Class* 10(4): 22–37.

———. 2006. "Color Blindness: An Obstacle to Racial Justice." Pp. 182–204 in *Mixed Messages: Multiracial Identities in the "Color-Blind" Era*. Edited by David Brunsma. Boulder, CO: Lynne Rienner.

Gans, Herbert. 1979. "Symbolic Ethnicity: The Future of Ethnic Groups and Cultures in America." *Ethnic and Racial Studies* 2: 1–19.

———. 1999. "The Possibility of a New Racial Hierarchy in the Twenty-First Century United States." Pp. 371–390 in *The Cultural Territories of Race*. Edited by Michele Lamont. Chicago and New York: University of Chicago Press and Russell Sage Foundation.

George, Rosemary Marangoly. 1997. "From Expatriate Aristocrat to Immigrant 'Nobody': South Asian Racial Strategies in the Southern California Context." *Diaspora* 6(1): 31–60.

Giroux, Henry A. 1983. *Theory and Resistance in Education*. London, England: Heinemann Educational Books.

Glazer, Nathan, and Daniel P. Moynihan. 1963. *Beyond the Melting Pot*. Cambridge, MA: MIT Press and Harvard University Press.

Golash-Boza, Tanya. 2006. "Dropping the Hyphen? Becoming Latino(a)-American Through Racialized Assimilation." *Social Forces* 85(1): 27–54.

Gomez, Christina. 1998. "The Racialization of Latinos in the United States: Racial Options in a Changing Society." PhD dissertation, 59 (5).

Goode, Judith, and Jo Anne Schneider. 1994. *Reshaping Ethnic and Racial Relations in Philadelphia: Immigrants in a Divided City*. Philadelphia: Temple University Press.

Gordon, Linda. 1999. *The Great Arizona Orphan Abduction*. Cambridge, MA: Harvard University Press.

Gossett, Thomas 1965. *Race: The History of an Idea in America*. Dallas, TX: Southern Methodist University Press.

Gramsci, Antonio. 1999/1971. *Selections from Prison Notebooks*. New York: International.

Hacker, Andrew. 1992. *Two Nations*. New York: Scribner.

Hale, Grace Elizabeth. 1998. *Making Whiteness: The Culture of Segregation in the South, 1890–1940*. New York: Random House.

Haney Lopez, Ian. 1996. *White By Law: The Legal Construction of Race*. New York: New York University Press.

———. 1999. "The Social Construction of Race." Pp. 163–175 in *Critical Race Theory: The Cutting Edge*. Edited by Richard Delgado and Jean Stafancic. Philadelphia: Temple University Press.

Harris, Cheryl. 1993. "Whiteness as Property." *Harvard Law Review* 106: 1707.

Harris, David. 1995. "Exploring the Determinants of Adult Black Identity: Context and Process." *Social Forces* 74: 227–241.

Harrison, Faye. 1991. "Ethnography as Politics." Pp. 88–109 in *Decolonizing Anthropology: Moving Towards an Anthropology for Liberation*. Edited by Faye Harrison. Washington, DC: Association of Black Anthropologists, American Anthropology Association.

Helms, Janet, ed. 1990. *Black and White Racial Identity: Theory, Research, and Practice*. Westport, CT: Greenwood Press.

Henry, P. J., and David Sears. 2002. "The Symbolic Racism 2000 Scale." *Political Psychology* 23(2): 253–283.

Herrnstein, Richard, and Charles Murray. 1994. *Bell Curve: Intelligence and Class Structure*. New York: Free Press.

Hill Collins, Patricia. 2000. *Black Feminist Thought: Knowledge, Consciousness, and the Politics of Empowerment*. New York: Routledge.

Hochschild, Jennifer. 1996. *Facing Up to the American Dream*. Princeton, NJ: Princeton University Press.

Hondagneu-Sotelo, Pierrette. 1994. *Gendered Transitions: Mexican Experiences of Immigration*. Berkeley: University of California Press.

hooks, bell. 1992. *Black Looks: Race and Representation*. Boston: South End Press.

Hughes, Michael. 1998. "Symbolic Racism, Old-Fashioned Racism, and Whites' Opposition to Affirmative Action." Pp. 45–75 in *Racial Attitudes in the 1990's*. Edited by Steven A. Tuch and Jack K. Martin. Westport, CT: Draeger.

Hughes, Michael, and Steven Tuch. 2000. "How Beliefs About Poverty Influence Racial Policy Attitudes." Pp. 165–190 in *Racialized Politics: The Debate About Racism in America*. Edited by David O. Sears, Jim Sidanius, and Lawrence Bobo. Chicago: University of Chicago Press.

Ignatiev, Noel. 1995. *How the Irish Became White*. New York: Routledge.

Ikemoto, Lisa C. 2000. "Traces of the Master Narrative in the Story of African American/Korean American Conflict: How We Constructed 'Los Angeles.'" Pp. 302–312 in *Critical Race Theory*. Edited by Richard Delgado and Jean Stefancic. Philadelphia: Temple University Press.

Islam, Naheed. 2000. "Research as an Act of Betrayal: Researching Race in an Asian Community in Los Angeles." Pp. 35–66 in *Racing Research, Researching Race*. Edited by France Winddance Twine and Jonathan W. Warren. New York: New York University Press.

Iszigsohn, Jose, and Carlos Dore Cabral. 2000. "Competing Identities? Race,

Ethnicity and Panethnicity Among Dominicans in the United States." *Sociological Forum* 15(2): 225–247.

Jacobson, Matthew Frye. 1998. *Whiteness of a Different Color: European Immigrants and the Alchemy of Race*. Cambridge, MA: Harvard University Press.

Jenson, Leif, and Yoshimi Chitose. 1994. "Today's Second Generation: Evidence from the 1990 U.S. Census." *International Migration Review* 28: 690–713.

Jo, Moon H. 1992. "Korean Merchants in the Black Community: Prejudice Among the Victims of Prejudice." *Ethnic and Racial Studies* 15(3): 395–411.

Johnson, James H., Walter Farrell, and Chandra Guinn. 1997. "Immigration Reform and the Browning of America: Tensions, Conflicts and Community Instability in Metropolitan Los Angeles." *International Migration Review* 31(4): 1055–1095.

Kahlenberg, Richard D. 1996. *The Remedy: Class, Race, and Affirmative Action*. New York: Basic Books.

Kasinitz, Philip. 1992. *Caribbean New York: Black Immigrants and the Politics of Race*. Ithaca, NY: Cornell University Press.

Kibria, Nazli. 1996. "Not Asian, Black or White? Reflections on South Asian American Racial Identity." *Amerasia Journal* 22(2): 77–86.

———. 1998. "The Contested Meanings of 'Asian American': Racial Dilemmas in the Contemporary U.S." *Ethnic and Racial Studies* 21(5): 939–958.

Kinder, Donald, and David O. Sears. 1981. "Prejudice and Politics: Symbolic Racism Versus Racial Threats to the Good Life." *Journal of Personality and Social Psychology* 40(3): 414–431.

Kinder, Donald, and Tali Mendelberg. 2000. "Individualism Reconsidered." Pp. 44–74 in *Racialized Politics: The Debate About Racism in America*. Edited by David O. Sears, Jim Sidanius, and Lawrence Bobo. Chicago: University of Chicago Press.

Kirschenman, Joleen, and Kathryn M. Neckerman. 1991. "We'd Love to Hire Them, but . . .: The Meaning of Race for Employers." *Social Problems* 38(4): 433–447.

Koshy, Susan. 1998. "Category Crisis: South Asian Americans and Questions of Race and Ethnicity." *Diaspora* 7(3): 285–320.

Kozol, Jonathan. 1991. *Savage Inequalities*. New York: HarperCollins.

———. 2006. "Segregated Schools: Shame of the City." *Gotham Gazette*. New York. Jan. 16.

Lampard, Richard. 2007. "Is Social Mobility an Echo of Educational Mobility? Parents' Educations and Occupations and Their Children's Occupational Attainment." *Sociological Research Online* 12(5).

Langston, Donna. 2001. "Tired of Playing Monopoly?" Pp. 126–136 in *Race, Class, and Gender: An Anthology*. Edited by Margaret L. Anderson and Patricia Hill Collins. Belmont, CA: Wadsworth.

Lee, Jennifer, Frank D. Bean, Jeanne Batalova, and Sabeen Sandhu. 2003. "Immigration and the Black-White Color Line in the United States." *Review of Black Political Economy* 31(1/2): 43–76.

Lee, Sharon. 1989. "Asian Immigration and American Race Relations: From Exclusion to Acceptance?" *Ethnic and Racial Studies* 12(3): 368–390.

Lee, Stacey J. 2005. *Up Against Whiteness: Race, School, and Immigrant Youth.* New York: Teacher's College Press.

Lieberson, Stanley. 1985. "Unhyphenated Whites in the United States." *Ethnic and Racial Studies* 8(1): 159–180.

Lipsitz, George. 1998. *The Possessive Investment in Whiteness: How White People Profit from Identity Politics.* Philadelphia: Temple University Press.

Logan, Enid. 1999. "El Apostol y el Comandante en Jefe: Dialectics of Racial Discourse and Racial Practice in Cuba, 1890–1999." *Research in Politics and Society* 6: 195–213.

Lomba-De-Andrade, Lelia. 2000. "Negotiating from the Inside: Constructing Ethnic Identity in Qualitative Research." *Journal of Contemporary Ethnography* 29(3): 268–290.

Lott, Juanita Tamayo. 1998. *Asian Americans: From a Racial Category to Multiple Identities.* Walnut Creek, CA: Alta Mira Press.

Lowe, Lisa. 1991. "Heterogeneity, Hybridity, Multiplicity: Marking Asian American Differences." *Diaspora* 1(1): 24–44.

———. 1996. *Immigrant Acts.* Durham, NC: Duke University Press.

Lubiano, Wahneema. 1992. "Black Ladies, Welfare Queens, and State Minstrels." Pp. 323–361 in *Race-ing Justice, En-gender-ing Power.* Edited by Toni Morrison. New York: Pantheon Books.

MacLeod, Jay. 1995. *Ain't No Makin' It: Aspirations and Attainment in a Low-Income Neighborhood.* Boulder, CO: Westview Press.

Mahler, Sarah J. 1995. *American Dreaming: Immigrant Life on the Margins.* Princeton, NJ: Princeton University Press.

Marx, Anthony. 1998. *Making Race and Nation: A Comparison of the United States, South Africa, and Brazil.* Cambridge: Cambridge University Press.

Massey, Douglas S., and Nancy A. Denton. 1993. *American Apartheid: Segregation and the Making of the Underclass.* Cambridge, MA: Harvard University Press.

Maxwell, Joseph. 1996. *Qualitative Research Design: An Interactive Approach.* Thousand Oaks, CA: Sage Publications.

McConahay, J. B., and J. C. Hough. 1976. "Symbolic Racism." *Journal of Social Issues* 32: 23–46.

Merton, Robert. 1972. "Insiders and Outsiders: A Chapter in the Sociology of Knowledge." *American Journal of Sociology* 78 (July): 9–47.

Miles, Jack. 1992. "Immigration and the New American Dilemma: Blacks vs. Browns." *The Atlantic* 27(4): 41–68.

Min, Pyong Gap and Rose Kim. 2000. "Formation of Ethnic and Racial Identities: Narratives by Young Asian-American Professionals." *Ethnic and Racial Studies* 23(4): 735–760.

Min, Pyong Gap and Rose Kim, eds. 1999. *Struggle for Ethnic Identity: Narratives by Asian American Professionals.* Walnut Creek, CA: Alta Mira Press.

Mohanty, Chandra Talpade. 2001. "On Being South Asian in North America." Pp. 336–342 in *Race, Class, and Gender in the United States.* Edited by Paula Rothenberg. New York: Worth.

Morgan, David L. 1988. *Focus Groups as Qualitative Research.* Newbury Park, CA: Sage Publications.

Morrison, Joan, and Charlotte Fox Zabusky, eds. 1980. *American Mosaic: The Immigrant Experience in the Words of Those Who Lived It.* Pittsburgh, PA: University of Pittsburgh Press.

Morrison, Toni. 1992. *Playing in the Dark: Whiteness and the Literary Imagination.* New York: Random House.

Neubeck, Kenneth J., and Noel A. Cazenave. 2001. *Welfare Racism: Playing the Race Card Against America's Poor.* New York: Routledge.

Newman, Katherine S. 1993. *Declining Fortunes: The Withering of the American Dream.* New York: Basic Books.

———. 1999. *Falling From Grace: Downward Mobility in the Age of Affluence.* Berkeley: University of California Press.

Nguyen, Ly Thi. 1998. "To Date or Not to Date a Vietnamese: Perceptions and Expectations of Vietnamese American College Students." *Amerasia Journal* 24(1): 143–169.

Ogbu, John U. 1990a. "Minority Education in Comparative Perspective. *Journal of Negro Education* 59(1): 45–57.

———. 1990b. "Minority Status and Literacy in Comparative Perspective. *Daedalus* 119(2): 141–168.

Ojanuga, Durrenda Nash. 1993. "The Ethiopian Jewish Experience as Blacks in Israel." *Journal of Black Studies* 24(2): 147–158.

Omi, Michael, and Howard Winant. 1994. *Racial Formation in the United States: From the 1960's to the 1990's.* New York: Routledge.

Ong, Aihwa. 1996. "Cultural Citizenship as Subject Making: Immigrants Negotiate Racial and Cultural Boundaries in the U.S." *Current Anthropology* 37(5): 737–762.

Pachon, Harry, and Louis DeSipio. 1994. *New Americans by Choice: Political Perspectives of Latino Immigrants.* Boulder, CO: Westview Press.

Palumbo-Liu, David. 1999. *Asian/American: Historical Crossings of a Racial Frontier.* Stanford, CA: Stanford University Press.

Park, Robert. 1950. *Race and Culture.* Glencoe, IL: Free Press.

Phinney, Jean S., and Mary Jane Rotheram. 1987. *Children's Ethnic Socialization: Pluralism and Development.* Newbury Park, CA: Sage Publications.

Piatt, Bill. 1997. *Black and Brown in America.* New York: New York University Press.

Piliawsky, Monte. 1998. "Remedies to De Facto School Segregation: The Case of Hartford." *Black Scholar* 28(2): 29–36.

Portes, Alejandro, ed. 1996. *The New Second Generation.* New York: Russell Sage Foundation.

Portes, Alejandro, Patricia Fernandez-Kelly, and William Haller. 2005. "Segmented Assimilation on the Ground: The New Second Generation in Early Adulthood." *Ethnic and Racial Studies* 28(6): 1000–1040.

Portes, Alejandro, and Dag MacLeod. 1996. "What Shall I Call Myself? Hispanic Identity Formation in the Second Generation." *Ethnic and Racial Studies* 19(3): 539–559.

Portes, Alejandro, and Ruben G. Rumbaut. 2001. *Legacies: The Story of the Immigrant Second Generation.* Berkeley: University of California Press.

Portes, Alejandro, and Min Zhou. 1993. "The New Second Generation: Segmented Assimilation and Its Variants." *Annals of the American Academy of Political & Social Science* 530: 74–97.

Premdas, Ralph R. 1995. "Racism and Anti-Racism in the Caribbean." Pp. 241–260 in *Racism and Anti-Racism in World Perspective*. Edited by Benjamin Bowser. Thousand Oaks, CA: Sage Publications.

Quintana, Stephen M., and Elizabeth M. Vera. 1999. "Mexican American Children's Ethnic Identity, Understanding of Ethnic Prejudice, and Parental Ethnic Socialization." *Hispanic Journal of Behavioral Sciences* 21(4): 387–404.

Rhodes, Penny J. 1994. "Race-of-Interviewer Effects: A Brief Comment." *Sociology: The Journal of the British Sociological Association* 28(2): 547–548.

Richmond, Anthony. 1990. "Race Relations and Immigration: A Comparative Perspective." *International Journal of Comparative Sociology* 31(3–4): 156–176.

Riggs, Marlon. 1986. *Ethnic Notions*. San Francisco: California Newsreel.

Rodriguez, Clara. 2000. *Changing Race: Latinos, the Census, and the History of Ethnicity in the United States*. New York: New York University Press.

Rodriguez, Joseph. 1998. "How Mexicans Became Mexican Americans: Recent Studies of Immigration, Labor, and Ethnic Identities." *Journal of Urban History* 24(4): 542–551.

Roediger, David. 1991. *The Wages of Whiteness*. London: Verso.

Rubin, Herbert J., and Irene S. Rubin. 1995. *Qualitative Interviewing: The Art of Hearing Data*. Thousand Oaks, CA: Sage Publications.

Sanchez, George. 1997. "Face the Nation: Race, Immigration, and the Rise of Nativism in Late Twentieth Century America." *International Migration Review* 31(4): 1009–1030.

Schaefer, Richard. 2005. *Race and Ethnicity in the United States*. New York: Prentice Hall.

Shuman, Howard, Charlotte Steeh, and Lawrence Bobo. 1985. *Racial Attitudes in America: Trends and Interpretations*. Cambridge, MA: Harvard University Press.

Smedley, Audrey. 1992. *Race in North America: Origin and Evolution of a Worldview*. Boulder, CO: Westview Press.

———. 1998. "'Race' and the Construction of Human Identity." *American Anthropologist* 100(3): 690–702.

Sowell, Thomas. 1981. *Ethnic America: A History*. New York: Basic Books.

Steinberg, Stephen. 1989. *The Ethnic Myth*. Boston: Beacon Press.

Stryker, Sheldon. 1991. "Exploring the Relevance of Social Cognition for the Relationship of Self and Society: Linking the Cognitive Perspective and Identity Theory." Pp. 19–42 in *The Self-Society Dynamic*. Edited by Judith A. Howard and Peter L. Callero. Cambridge: Cambridge University Press.

Suarez-Orozco, Carola, and Marcelo Suarez-Orozco. 2001. *Children of Immigration*. Cambridge, MA: Harvard University Press.

Suro, Roberto. 1998. *Strangers Among Us: How Latino Immigration is Transforming America*. New York: Alfred A. Knopf.

Swift, Mike. 2001. "Bosnia Square." *Hartford Courant*. December 9: *Northeast Magazine*.

Tatum, Beverly Daniel. 1994. "Teaching White Students About Racism: The Search for White Allies and the Restoration of Hope." *Teachers College Record* 95(4): 462–476.

Thomas, W. I., and Florian Znaniecki. 1923. *The Polish Peasant in Europe and America*. New York: Knopf.

Tilove, Jonathan. 2001. "Racial Relations Becoming More Complex Across Country." Pp. 119–124 in *Race, Class, and Gender in the United States*. Edited by Paula Rothenberg. New York: Worth.

Tuan, Mia. 1998. *Forever Foreigners or Honorary Whites? The Asian Ethnic Experience Today*. New Brunswick, NJ: Rutgers University Press.

Tuch, Steven A., and Jack K. Martin, eds. 1998. *Racial Attitudes in the 1990's*. Westport, CT: Draeger.

Van Ausdale, Debra, and Joe R. Feagin. 2001. *The First R: How Children Learn Race and Racism*. Lanham, MD: Rowman and Littlefield.

van Dijk, Teun A. 1987. *Communicating Racism: Ethnic Prejudice and Thought and Talk*. Newbury Park, CA: Sage Publications.

———. 1993. *Elite Discourse and Racism*. Newbury Park, CA: Sage Publications.

———, ed. 1985. *Handbook of Discourse Analysis*. Vol. 4. London: Academic Press.

Vickerman, Milton. 1999. *Crosscurrents: West Indian Immigrants and Race*. New York: Oxford University Press.

Visweswaran, Kamala. 1997. "Diaspora By Design: Flexible Citizenship and South Asians in U.S. Racial Formation." *Diaspora* 6(1): 5–29.

Waldinger, Roger, and Cynthia Feliciano. 2004. "Will the New Second Generation Experience 'Downward Assimilation'? Segmented Assimilation Re-Assessed." *Ethnic and Racial Studies* 27(3): 376–402.

Waters, Mary. 1990. *Ethnic Options: Choosing Identities in America*. Berkeley, CA: University of California Press.

———. 1994. "Ethnic and Racial Identities of Second Generation Black Immigrants in New York City." *International Migration Review* 28(4): 795–820.

———. 1999. *Black Identities: West Indian Immigrant Dreams and American Realities*. New York: Russell Sage Foundation.

Watkins-Owens, Irma. 1996. *Blood Relations: Caribbean Immigrants and the Harlem Community, 1900–1930*. Bloomington: Indiana University Press.

Weitzer, Ronald. 1997. "Racial Prejudice Among Korean Merchants in African American Neighborhoods." *Sociological Quarterly* 38(4): 587–606.

West, Cornel. 1993. *Race Matters*. Boston: Beacon Press.

Williams, Teresa Kay, and Michael C. Thornton. 1998. "Social Construction of Ethnicity Versus Personal Experience: The Case of Afro-Amerasians." *Journal of Comparative Family Studies* 29(2): 255–267.

Willis, Paul E. 1978. *Learning to Labour: How Working Class Kids Get Working Class Jobs*. Westmead, England: Saxon House, Teakfield.

Wilson, Carter. 1996. *Racism: From Slavery to Advanced Capitalism*. Thousand Oaks, CA: Sage Publications.

Wilson, William J. 1978. *The Declining Significance of Race*. Chicago: Chicago University Press.

———. 1987. *The Truly Disadvantaged: The Inner City, the Underclass, and Public Policy*. Chicago: University of Chicago Press.

Winant, Howard. 1994. *Racial Conditions: Politics, Theory, Comparisons*. Minneapolis: University of Minnesota Press.

Winddance, Twine, Frances and Jonathan W. Warren, eds. 2000. *Racing Research, Researching Race*. New York: New York University Press.

Wu, F. H. 2002. *Yellow: Race in America Beyond Black and White*. New York: Basic Books.

X, Malcolm. 1992/1965. *The Autobiography of Malcolm X* (with the Assistance of Alex Haley). New York: Ballantine Books.

Yancey, George. 2003. *Who Is White? Latinos, Asians, and the New Black/Nonblack Divide*. Boulder, CO: Lynne Rienner.

———. 2006. "Racial Justice in a Black/Nonblack Society." Pp. 86–111 in *Mixed Messages: Multiracial Identities in the "Color-Blind" Era*. Edited by David Brunsma. Boulder, CO: Lynne Rienner.

Young, Jr., Alford A. 1999. "The (Non)Accumulation of Capital: Explicating the Relationship of Structure and Agency in the Lives of Poor Black Men." *Sociological Theory* 17(2): 201–227.

Zinn, Maxine Baca. 1979. "Field Research in Minority Communities: Ethical, Methodological and Political Observations by an Insider." *Social Problems* 27(2): 209–219.

Zhou, Min, and Yang Sao Xiong. 2005. "The Multifaceted American Experiences of the Children of Asian Immigrants: Lessons for Segmented Assimilation." *Ethnic and Racial Studies* 28(6): 1119–1152.

Zubrinsky, Camille L., and Lawrence Bobo. 1996. "Prismatic Metropolis: Race and Residential Segregation in the City of Angels." *Social Science Research* 25(4): 335–374.

Index

167

About the Book

With rising numbers of immigrants of color in the United States, sheer demographic change has long promised—falsely, it now seems—to solve the "race problem." Directly connecting the issues of race relations and immigrant incorporation, Beth Merenstein sheds light on what the changing contours of the United States racial and ethnic makeup mean for our dearly held concept of "equal opportunity for all."

Beth Frankel Merenstein is assistant professor of sociology at Central Connecticut State University.